MEN-AT-ARMS SERIES

EDITOR: PHILIP WARNER

The Arab Legion

Text by **BRIGADIER PETER YOUNG**
DSO, MC, MA, FSA, FRHist.S, FRGS

Colour plates by **MICHAEL ROFFE**

OSPREY PUBLISHING LIMITED

Published in England by
Osprey Publishing, Elms Court, Chapel Way,
Botley, Oxford OX2 9LP, United Kingdom.
© Copyright 1972 Osprey Publishing Ltd.
Email: info@ospreypublishing.com

Special Reprint 2002

I wish to record my gratitude to Major W.F.
Woodhouse, R.T.R., who has rendered me the
greatest assistance in preparing this work.
Commissioned in 1948, he served as a captain in the
Arab Legion from 1953 to 1956. He was Technical
Adjutant to the Armoured Brigade and then to the
3rd Tank Regiment, and his knowledge of the
weapons and vehicles of the Armoured Brigade has
been particularly helpful.

Since leaving the Legion he has qualified at the
Royal Military College of Science, and is currently
employed at the Military Vehicles and Engineering
Establishment. Like so many other British soldiers –
including myself – Bill Woodhouse looks back on
his three years with the Arab Legion as being
among the happiest in his Army career.

ISBN 0 85045 084 5

Printed in China through World Print Ltd.

Chronology

1920
October   Peake forms the Arab Legion.

1924   Defeat of the *Wahhabis* by R.A.F. at Ziza.

1927   Anglo-Transjordan Treaty and Legion establishment reduced.

1930   Glubb arrives to form the Desert Patrol.

1932
July   Last tribal raid.

1936   Arab rising in Palestine. Formation of Desert Mechanized Force.

1939   Campaign against Arab infiltraters from Palestine and Syria.
21 March   Peake retires.
3 September   Second World War begins.

1941
April   Campaign in Iraq. Desert Mechanized Regiment accompanies Habforce.
June   Syrian Campaign. Desert Mechanized Regiment again accompanies Habforce and plays a decisive part at Sukhna on 1 July.

1945   Second World War ends.

1946   New Anglo-Transjordan Treaty; Amir Abdallah becomes King of a truly independent state.
15 May   Palestine Mandate ends and Legion occupies Arab areas.

18 May   Arab Legion enters Jerusalem.
25 May–
11 June   Fighting round Latrun.
11 June–
9 July   Ceasefire, followed by further fighting round Latrun.

1949
3 April   Israeli-Transjordan Armistice signed.

1951   King Abdallah assassinated.

1953
14–15
October   The Qibya Incident.

1954   The Jerusalem Incident.
30 June–
2 July   The Beit Liqya Incident.

1955   Jordan application to join Baghdad Pact. Egyptian-inspired riots.

1956
1 March   Glubb and other British officers dismissed; Arab Legion becomes 'The Jordan Arab Army'.

Foreword

Writing these pages has revived memories of three very happy years spent in the Arab Legion, in the days when Glubb Pasha, already a legendary figure, was in command, and when Cooke Pasha was forging the 1st Division. Man for man the Arab Legion was the best of all the Arab armies. In 1967 the Jordanian Army, according to friend and foe alike, fought far better than the Egyptians or the Syrians. I look back with the greatest pleasure on the days when I commanded the 9th Regiment. Such opportunities do not come to the British officer of the present generation. The British Army need not be ashamed of the officers it sent to help with the expansion of the Arab Legion. Men like Galletly, Elliott, McCully, Hutton, Wormald, Leakey, Griffiths, and Tirrell, to name but a handful, had fought with the greatest distinction in the Second World War, and several went on to be major-generals in our own service. They were men who really had something to pass on. It was the policy of H.M. Government at that time to give Jordan military assistance. It would be a mistake, however, to suppose that this policy was directed against Israel. This was not the case. On the contrary the British officers, generally speaking, exercised a restraining influence. They were not quick on the trigger. British officers went to the Legion in the normal course of their careers, and for no ulterior motive. To serve in such an army and with such keen soldiers was sufficient privilege. To command a bedouin regiment was a magnificent experience.

To my former comrades of the Arab Legion – Arab, British and Circassian – I dedicate this book.

Al Jeish Al Arabi

The end of the First World War in 1918 brought not only peace to the former Turkish possessions in the Middle East but administrative chaos. The situation was not eased when in 1920 the French, as the mandatory power, demanded the withdrawal of British troops from Syria; the British not only complied, but withdrew at the same time from Transjordan, leaving the country east of the River Jordan without effective government.

The opponents of the French occupation of Syria soon took advantage of this situation to use Transjordan as a base of operations, and in 1921 the Amir Abdallah appeared in Ma'an in southern Transjordan with a force of tribesmen determined to evict the French. However, as a result of the British Middle East Conference then meeting in Cairo conflict was averted and Abdallah was persuaded to accept the Amirate of Transjordan,

which was thus recognized as a state and part of the British mandated territories.

It was against this background that in October 1920 Captain F. G. Peake, who had recently been posted to the newly-formed Palestine Police, was sent across to Transjordan to report on the gendarmerie there. He found a small and totally inefficient force – 'the officers were of the coffee-house loafing class who seldom troubled to dress in uniform and the men were lazy and dissatisfied, having received no pay for many months'. It was immediately plain to Peake that nothing could be achieved without a properly disciplined force and he obtained authority to raise 100 men. The force was to be called *Al Jeish Al Arabi* – the title used by Feisal's forces, with whom Peake had served in the recent war. Though literally translated as 'The Arab Army' – a somewhat grandiose title for so small a force – the English version became 'The Arab Legion'.

The Arab Legion consisted initially of five officers, seventy-five cavalry and twenty-five mounted machine-gunners; its responsibilities were little more than the policing of Amman, the capital, and its immediate area. Shortly afterwards a further two officers and fifty men were raised for the Kerak area. The Legion had only been in existence for a few months when the first real setback occurred. In north-west Transjordan lay the country of El Kura, peopled by a peculiarly intractable tribe who refused to pay their taxes. The government in Amman, without so much as consulting Peake, sent off the entire Legion, under an Arab officer, to bring the recalcitrant tribesmen to heel. This officer unhesitatingly marched his men into a deep *wadi* where they were successfully ambushed, the force losing eighteen killed, a large number wounded and all its horses. The survivors dispersed to their homes in shame.

Undismayed, Peake set about reforming his discredited force. Somewhat reluctantly eight of his best men agreed to come back, and as time passed a few more recruits trickled in. These men provided the nucleus when, in late 1921, Peake was ordered to increase the Legion's strength to about 750 men. Peake's persuasive powers overcame the initial reluctance of the local people to enlist, and it soon became a question of turning away the eager applicants. The Arab Legion now became organized into two companies of infantry, two squadrons of cavalry, a troop of artillery and a signals section. For reasons of economy the civil police also were placed under control of Arab Legion Headquarters so that the whole command numbered some 1,300 men.

The next few years demonstrated Peake's ability both as a soldier and an administrator, for the standard of the Arab Legion improved and the country became more peaceful. One serious problem, however, remained. In the mid-1920s when the Legion was beginning to deal effectively with the periodic disturbances in the settled areas, a more serious threat grew up. This was the *Wahhabi* movement, a Muslim religious revival in what is now Saudi Arabia. The *Ikhwan*, or brethren, were determined to convert the people of Transjordan by the sword. Their efforts were thwarted at Ziza in 1924, by an R.A.F. force based on Amman, a battle in which the Arab Legion took little part; however, the threat resulted in the formation of the Transjordan Frontier Force which, when the Anglo-Transjordan treaty was signed in 1927, assumed responsibility for maintaining the frontier. It was responsible direct to the High Commissioner for Palestine. The treaty recognized Transjordan's 'independence', while giving Great Britain the responsibility for external defence and foreign relations. The effect of all this was another blow to the Arab Legion, which suffered a reduction of 600 men, including the loss of its artillery and signals. Henceforth the Legion's rôle was to be confined to internal security.

Peake had recruited the Legion, quite deliberately, from the village Arabs or *haderi*, because he saw the encroachment of the bedouin on the cultivated areas as the greatest threat to stable and prosperous Arab government. Initially this worked reasonably well, but with the rise to power of Ibn Saud in Saudi Arabia the inter-tribal raiding, which had always characterized bedouin life, assumed an international status, since it disregarded the borders of the two new states. It became necessary to deal with the nomad tribes, but this neither the Transjordan Frontier Force, whose task it properly was, nor the reconstituted Arab Legion could do.

The need for some sort of desert police was

Sergeant Ismahil Abu Karachi of the Desert Patrol photographed on 30 October 1944. (Imperial War Museum)

evident and when, in December 1930, Peake asked for assistance, Major J. B. Glubb, M.C., was sent to him from Iraq, where he had already been serving with distinction amongst the bedouin. Glubb started to raise the Desert Patrol (the *Badieh*) from among the nomad tribes themselves; the beginnings were small, since it was only by personal persuasion that he was able to get anyone to join him at all. His first patrol consisted of himself, his driver, Alec Kirkbride the Assistant British Resident in Amman, and the Amir Saaker Ibn Zeid, president of the Bedouin Control Board. However, as Glubb's reputation spread, recruits from the tribes gradually came in, and by April 1931 the *Badieh* had been able to take over from the Transjordan Frontier Force both the Bair and Mudowwara sectors – in each case with a very small detachment. So effective were Glubb's methods that within a year virtually all tribal raiding had ceased and the last raid in the desert took place in July 1932. Even the Howeitat – the principal offenders on the Saudi frontier – after an initial reluctance began to join the Desert Patrol, and Glubb's command was soon up to its

Cap badge, Regular Army. The silver cap badge of the Arab Legion is the same for soldiers and police, but the National Guard have a different badge in yellow metal

full strength of ninety men. Detachments, camel-mounted, lived on their own in their patrol areas, often commanded by a son of the local sheikh, and before long it became an honour to belong to the *Badieh*, whose morale was correspondingly high.

The period 1932 to 1936 was one of steady, and generally peaceful, progress. Glubb continued in command of the Desert Patrol, under the overall direction of Peake, who himself remained at the head of affairs in Amman. The relationship of both men with the Amir Abdallah and his Government became increasingly cordial.

In 1936 the Arab rising in Palestine began and though its effects were little felt in Transjordan to start with, it soon became clear that some central reserve was needed to meet the threat to security from across the border. From 1930 the entire strength of the Legion had been deployed around the country in small detachments. Now a reserve of two squadrons of horsed cavalry and the Desert Mechanized Force of 350 bedouin soldiers mounted in trucks was raised and trained. The wisdom of this decision was evident when in March 1939 a para-military force some 100 strong entered the country from Syria. It was spotted heading towards the wooded Ajlun mountains, but before it could reach the hills was engaged by the Desert Mechanized Force, whose first action

this was, under command of a recently joined British officer, Lieutenant Macadam. The bedouin dashed into action and soon gained the upper hand. R.A.F. aircraft from Amman arrived to give support, pressing home their attack so successfully that the enemy broke up in panic. The raiders suffered some thirty-five casualties, the rest vanishing under cover of darkness. The Arab Legion lost its new British officer and one sergeant killed and three other ranks wounded.

The March engagement set the scene for a series of similar incursions over the next few weeks, but the Legion soon got the measure of their opponents and on 24 April a final action was fought at Beit Idis. Here a force of some 200 guerrillas were surprised by the horsed cavalry and the Desert Mechanized Force. A running fight ensued as the enemy were pursued into the wooded hills above the village; contact was finally lost in the early evening, the enemy having suffered about eleven killed and at least twenty wounded. This action finally discouraged the guerrilla leaders, and their bands of infiltraters were seen no more in Transjordan. On 21 March 1939 Glubb had assumed command of the Arab Legion when Peake retired and returned to England. As Glubb himself says, '. . . a considerable portion of the people of Transjordan were scarcely able to remember the days before Colonel Peake came. His disappearance from the scene marked the end of an epoch for the Arab Legion, and indeed for Transjordan itself.'

The outbreak of war in Europe found Transjordan in an uneasy lull following the campaign against the Palestinian guerrillas. While the cavalry patrolled the Syrian and Palestine borders, the Desert Mechanized Force, now augmented by six locally-made armoured cars, continued its interrupted training. Just before war was declared Captain N. O. Lash joined Glubb as the only other British officer, and took over command of the Desert Patrol.

On the outbreak of war in 1939 the Amir Abdallah gave an unhesitating pledge of full support for Great Britain. This was not taken very seriously until after the fall of France in 1940, when the Germans and Italians began to arrive to take over the Syrian and Lebanese Governments. With the British Army in Egypt committed to the Western Desert, the tiny Arab Legion immediately assumed an importance beyond its size: it was indeed practically the sole defence against any invasion from the east. It was decided that the Desert Mechanized Force should be enlarged to form a Mechanized Regiment, which the British agreed to equip. Meanwhile, German influence in Syria and Iraq increased and in early 1941 a *coup d'état* took place in Baghdad where a pro-German party seized power; in April the régime declared war on Great Britain and a force was accordingly gathered together in Palestine to cross the desert and relieve the besieged British garrison of the Habbaniyah R.A.F. station. Glubb, accompanied by Lash and the Mechanized Regiment, was to accompany 'Habforce', with the task on arrival in Iraq of contacting loyal elements and persuading them to rise against the régime.

The Mechanized Regiment (still in fact the 350 men of the original Mechanized Force, since the promised new equipment had not yet arrived) was ordered to cover the concentration of 'Habforce' at H4, a station on the Iraq Petroleum Company's pipeline, and, if possible, to capture the frontier post fort at Rutbah, held by some 100 Iraqi police. On the morning of 8 May the Legion invested the fort but, despite some desultory bombing by a single R.A.F. aircraft, the Iraqis showed no inclination to surrender. Without artillery or mortars the Legion was powerless and when at dusk on the second day a large vehicle convoy appeared with reinforcements for the garrison, the Mechanized Regiment was forced to withdraw to H3 in order to replenish with water and ammunition. Meanwhile, an R.A.F. armoured car company, supported from the air, renewed the attack to such good effect that on 10 May the garrison abandoned the fort.

The Legion now prepared to accompany 'Kingcol', the flying column commanded by Brigadier Kingstone, on its dash to relieve Habbaniyah. It seems clear that at this time neither Kingstone nor Major-General Clarke, Habforce commander, fully appreciated the potential of the Legion force accompanying them. However, when most of Kingcol's vehicles bogged down in the soft sand and there was gloomy talk of returning to Rutbah, Glubb managed to persuade the Brigadier that his experienced desert

Trooper of Glubb's Desert Patrol camelry. Glubb Pasha formed the Desert Patrol in 1931 from among the bedouin to put an end to raiding by nomadic tribesmen

soldiers could show them the way. Guided by the Legion, the whole force moved into Habbaniyah without difficulty and unopposed. The only casualties occurred in the rearguard which was attacked by four German fighters; two bedouin soldiers fought back gallantly with the Lewis gun mounted in their truck, one being killed and one badly wounded.

After the relief of Habbaniyah the Mechanized Regiment was employed in raids on the Jezireh area north of Mosul in an effort to cut the Mosul-Baghdad railway, Glubb at the same time making such local contacts as he could. The Legion also reconnoitred suitable routes for the attack on Baghdad, and the columns which advanced on the city towards the end of May were all led by Arab Legion guides. By 31 May the outskirts of the city had been reached and the Iraqis had requested an armistice, the terms of which Glubb helped to draft. Habforce entered Baghdad on 1 June and on 2 June the Arab Legion Mechanized Regiment, its job done, set out across the desert to return to Amman.

Chevrolet trucks of the Arab Legion Desert Mechanized Force, which took part in the Syrian campaign, lined up on the parade ground for inspection by the Amir. Each truck carries a Lewis gun, and the crew of five and one driver carry rifles and revolvers. (Imperial War Museum)

The Legion did not have long to recuperate. Operations to forestall any German occupation of Syria began on 10 June, though initially without the support of the Arab Legion. However, on 21 June Habforce was withdrawn from Iraq and it and the Mechanized Regiment were ordered into Syria, with Palmyra as their objective. Major-General Clarke's force was divided into three columns. The Royal Wiltshire Yeomanry led the way, guided by an Arab Legion detachment; their task to capture the hills west of Palmyra. The remainder of 4th Cavalry Brigade, again guided by a Legion detachment, were to move east of the town and capture the northern hills. The third column, which included Force Headquarters, consisted of the 1st Essex, some artillery and sappers and five Arab Legion troops led by Glubb; the Legion's task after the attack on Palmyra being to cover the rear of British troops moving west towards Homs.

It had been hoped that Palmyra would fall on the first day but surprise was lost at Juffa, some

twenty-five miles to the south-east, when a Vichy post managed to get off a radio message before it was overrun by the Yeomanry. In addition, 4th Cavalry Brigade was held up at T3, an Iraq Petroleum Company cantonment. Leaving a party to watch the French garrison at T3, the rest of Habforce moved on to attack Palmyra, under continual French air attack. On 26 June, with the main force investing Palmyra, the Legion was ordered to capture Seba' Biyar to the east and then to take Sukhna, some thirty miles to the north-east, in order to secure the lines of communication. Soon after dawn on 28 June Glubb's force approached Seba' Biyar, which surrendered as the force drove up – just as well since the attackers had no artillery.

On 29 June the Legion moved out to Sukhna and found the village unoccupied by the enemy. However, early on 1 July a column was observed approaching from Deir ez Zor while most of the troops were away getting breakfast. Leaving Lash with the Legion's three armoured cars and a troop of infantry, in a position he had prepared on a hill to the east of the village, Glubb went off to alert the Household Cavalry squadron which had joined his force two days before, and sent a truck to recall his own troops. On his return he found Lash already engaged with French infantry and armoured cars; the bedouin infantry, never patient of a defensive battle, could not restrain themselves and, instead of holding on until the remainder of the force could take the French in the flank, as Glubb had ordered, rushed into the attack. Although greatly outnumbered they pressed home their assault with dash and gallantry, and, supported by the three armoured cars, put the enemy to flight. The French vehicles made off to the east. Fortunately the Legion's infantry trucks appeared at that moment and Glubb instantly gave chase. The French inadvertently ran into a dried-up watercourse, were caught and surrendered without further fighting. Only one vehicle escaped.

The French troops at Sukhna consisted of 2nd Light Desert Company and when their comrades in Palmyra heard what had happened they mutinied and forced their officers to surrender. By 11 July the fighting in Syria was over, the battle at Sukhna having been instrumental in achieving this result. The signal sent by General Wilson, G.O.C. Palestine, to the Amir Abdallah on 2 July expressed well the high esteem in which the Legion was held – 'The Transjordan Desert Patrol [sic], under Glubb Pasha, carried out yesterday at Sukhna, a most successful operation, capturing 80 prisoners, 6 armoured cars and 12 machine guns. I offer respectful congratulations on spirited action and fighting qualities of your troops.'

Sukhna was destined to be the last action fought by the Legion in the Second World War; despite persistent efforts by Glubb and the Amir Abdallah to persuade the British to employ the Legion in an active rôle, the years till 1945 were spent in furnishing guard companies for installations throughout the Middle East theatre. During the war years the Legion expanded to three infantry regiments with a brigade headquarters, formed for operations which never in fact materialized, in addition to the sixteen guard companies dispersed about the theatre.

The year 1946 was marked by the negotiation of a new treaty with Britain, under which Transjordan became truly independent and the Amir became King Abdallah. However, more serious work lay ahead, for two years later, on 15 May 1948, the Palestine Mandate was due to end; in response to the pleas of the Palestinians, who had no other forces to protect them against the Jews, Transjordan prepared to occupy with the Arab Legion those areas of Palestine adjacent to her frontiers which had been allocated to the Arabs. The troops available for this operation consisted of four lorried infantry battalions organized in two brigades, plus two batteries of 25-pounder guns, four guns to each battery. There were in addition seven garrison companies who had had little tactical training and possessed no support weapons. The total strength was about 4,500 all ranks and was commanded by Brigadier Lash with an improvised headquarters, under the overall direction of Glubb Pasha. There were no reserves of trained men and little beyond first line stocks of mortar and artillery ammunition.

On 15 May the Arab Legion crossed into Palestine; 1 Brigade (1st and 3rd Regiments) moved to the Nablus area, while 3 Brigade (so-called for deception) consisting of 2nd and 4th Regiments moved to Ramallah; both brigades were soon involved in a number of small actions as the Jews moved forward into the Arab areas. Meanwhile the U.N. Truce Committee tried to stop the fighting which had already started in the supposedly internationalized Jerusalem. Glubb was reluctant to move into the Holy City while truce negotiations continued but, appreciating that the Jews there were being reinforced from Tel Aviv, 4th Regiment was moved to Latrun to block that route. At noon on 17 May Glubb received a direct order from King Abdallah to move the army into Jerusalem where the Jews appeared to be gaining the upper hand; Glubb still hoped to avoid the action, knowing that his slender force would be stretched beyond its limit if fully committed to street fighting in addition to its commitments elsewhere in Palestine. Nevertheless, on 18 May he ordered 1st Independent Company to move forward from the Mount of Olives and man the Old City walls.

Although the presence of the Legion in Jerusalem stiffened Arab resistance it was clearly not enough, and on 19 May Lash was ordered to break into the city from the north with whatever troops he could muster. By clearing the Sheikh Jarrah area and establishing a line across the western edge of the Old City, Glubb hoped to halt the Jewish offensive. The attack went in at 03·45 hours on 19 May and consisted of one infantry company, one armoured car squadron (at that time an integral part of each lorried infantry battalion), four 6-pounder anti-tank guns and four 3-inch mortars. There was also limited support from one battery of artillery. This small force of 300 men, reinforced during the day by two more companies, was firmly established in Sheikh Jarrah by nightfall, although the armoured cars had had to withdraw. The next day this *ad hoc* collection of troops continued to hold on under mounting enemy pressure and Lash decided to relieve them with 3rd Regiment, the only unit available. This meant virtually denuding Samaria of troops, but with no alternative now that the Legion was committed to the battle for Jerusalem, the order was given and shortly after 04·00 hours on 21 May the Regiment came into action.

For several hours the fighting was confused and intense and it was not until 14·00 hours that the

Troopers of the Household Cavalry Squadron parading before setting out on patrol. October 1944. (Imperial War Museum)

companies had reached their positions near Notre Dame – from which the Jews dominated the whole area. This strongpoint had to be taken before a proper defensive line could be established and on 23 May an attempt was made, but progress was slow. Fighting continued throughout that day and night and through the following day. Although 3rd Regiment gained a foothold in the immense block of buildings which made up Notre Dame, they were unable to hold on and casualties were mounting: at 17.00 hours on 24 May the attack was abandoned. The Regiment had fought bravely, but was now exhausted and casualties could not be replaced. Nevertheless, the Old City was held and that had been the main objective. Meanwhile two independent infantry companies were now heavily committed inside the Old City,

fighting off attacks from Mount Zion to the south and at the same time attacking the Jewish quarter within the walls, an area which was not cleared until 28 May.

The main action now swung to Latrun, where 4th Infantry Regiment had been blocking the Tel Aviv road since 15 May. From 25 May until 11 June Jewish pressure on this vital position increased. Nevertheless 4th Regiment, later reinforced by 2nd Regiment, held firm against all attacks, the Jews losing hundreds of men in fruitless assaults on Latrun itself, at Bab Al Wad and on Radar, this last position having been wrested from them by 1st Regiment in a brilliant attack on 26 May.

Meanwhile Count Bernadotte, the U.N. mediator, had arranged a truce for 11 June but this lasted barely a month, the Arab leaders deciding to renew the fighting on 9 July. The resumption of hostilities found the Legion's 3 Brigade in the Latrun area, with its right flank weakly covered by the Arab-held towns of Ramle and Lydda; the Jews planned to attack this vulnerable area with the Palmach, their *corps d'élite* some 6,500 strong, and then capture Latrun itself from the 1,500 men of the Arab Legion who held it. Lydda and Ramle, garrisoned by irregulars, fell to the Jews on 12 July and on 15 July they attempted to outflank the Latrun position from the north. They were, however, held at Al Burj by a 2nd Regiment counterattack. Fighting continued in the area until 18 July, when the Palmach put in a final effort supported by armour; almost all their tanks were knocked out by a gallantly-served 6-pounder and the infantry attack never materialized. Latrun was held.

Bernadotte had arranged for another truce to take effect on 18 July and this lasted, with a number of violations, until October, despite the tension caused by the Jewish assassination of Bernadotte on 17 September. However, on 15 October the Egyptians were defeated in the Neqev by a large-scale Jewish attack which cut off from the rest of their army the Egyptians in Hebron. A small detachment of the Legion moved into the area just in time to stave off a determined Jewish armoured car attack, and thus undoubtedly saved Hebron itself and the surrounding area for the Arabs.

By November 1948 only the Arab Legion and the Iraqi army remained in the field, with the Legion holding a 100-mile front with, by this time, some 10,000 men. An uneasy cease-fire prevailed until 3 April 1949 when an Israeli-Transjordan Armistice was finally signed in Rhodes.

Although the fighting officially ended with the Rhodes Armistice, for the Arab Legion, faced with the responsibility of guarding a 400-mile frontier (the Iraqis having withdrawn) against an aggressive enemy, 'peace' was a relative term. Apart from its operational task the Legion had an enormous training problem. During the fighting the army had expanded, in somewhat haphazard fashion, from a strength of 6,000 to some 12,000 men; the *ad hoc* divisional organization which had

been used in the 1948 fighting had to be put on a more permanent basis and the need for administrative units was painfully obvious. At the same time the Legion had a great lack of senior officers, particularly in the technical arms; if the army was to become a modern and up-to-date fighting force it needed the technical equipment and experienced officers to train the soldiers in the handling and use of it. The only source of such aid was the British Government, which already provided a subsidy, eventually totalling some ten million pounds a year; and this at a time when, somewhat paradoxically, most Palestinian Arabs saw the British as the author of all their misfortunes. Understandably, as the British element in the Legion increased, so did the people of Jordan – which now included a large slice of Palestine and a vast number of refugees – begin to question British involvement in Jordanian affairs. However, despite frontier incidents and despite the assassination of King Abdallah in 1951, to be succeeded after Tallal's brief reign by the Amir Hussein in 1952, Jordan remained outwardly calm and the army steadfastly loyal. Glubb himself was well aware of these under-currents, and plans were made for the gradual handover of British command to Arabs, as the latter gradually became qualified – more or less – for high command. The process was too slow for Arab tastes.

Meanwhile, from 1949, when 1 Division (of three brigades) was formed from the nine infantry regiments which had grown up during 1948, rapid expansion took place. Lash, the first divisional commander, retired in 1951 to be succeeded by Major-General Cooke, who remained with the Legion until 1956. In 1951 also, the armoured car squadrons, which had formed part of the infantry battalions, were collected into an armoured car regiment, the nucleus of an armoured force which later included a regiment of tanks. The artillery was similarly expanded to provide a field regiment for each infantry brigade, a light anti-aircraft regiment and an anti-tank regiment. Engineers and service units also appeared gradually, while the signals expanded to form a regiment; at the same time, though there was little money to pay for it, a National Guard was formed to provide some sort of reserve and to enable the frontier villages to protect themselves.

Captain Mohammed inspects infantry at the Arab Legion Training School, October 1944. (Imperial War Museum)

Until 1953 only one of the three brigades was stationed on the West Bank, as that area of Palestine which the Arab Legion had held for the Arabs came to be known; the remainder were mostly based on Zerka and Khaw, north of Amman, and Irbid, and were kept busy training. In October of that year, however, an incident occurred at the village of Qibya, about ten miles north of Latrun, which altered the situation dramatically. An attack on the village by the Israeli army in battalion strength resulted in the destruction of Qibya itself and the slaughter of some sixty-eight people, mostly women and children. To make matters worse, no effective counter action was taken by the brigade stationed in the area. The result of this disastrous incident was that from then on two infantry brigades were permanently stationed on the West Bank and training of the division suffered in consequence. One brigade was kept around Jerusalem and the other near Nablus. The incident at Qibya also led to serious riots in Amman, which were suppressed without bloodshed by the 2nd Armoured Car Regiment and the 9th (Infantry) Regiment.

Qibya heralded a change of policy on the part of the Israelis. General Dayan, who had recently become Chief of Staff, was now in power. In his book 200 black rabbits made a black horse. That is to say that when there had been a number of cases of infiltration from Egypt, Jordan or Syria it was his policy to strike a massive blow in return. This had the added advantage of giving his picked troops, led by men like Sharon and Davidi, a great deal of experience in night operations and raiding at which they came to excel. That some of the Arab infiltration was done by guerrillas is not unlikely, but it must be remembered that *El Fatah* and the *fedayeen* had not really got going in 1953. Most of the infiltraters were dispossessed Palestinians going across the border to see their friends and relations; a few were smugglers.

The attack on Qibya underlined the need for effective tactics which, if they could not deter the Israelis from attacking, could at least prevent the enemy escaping afterwards and perhaps discourage them from trying again. Israeli 'reprisal raids' of varying intensity continued to occur throughout 1954. The improved ability of the Legion to cope with this kind of warfare, no small part of which consisted of preventing Jordanians from infiltrating into Israel, was demonstrated at Beit Liqya, four miles inside Jordan, in September 1954. The village was attacked by about two companies of Israelis, but on this occasion the National Guard, under a regular N.C.O., repulsed the attack. The Israelis, knowing that Legion reinforcements could be expected, had mined the likely approach roads and covered them with ambush parties. Sure enough a Legion platoon moving down one route ran into the ambush and was halted. A company of 7th Regiment, however, encountering a second Israeli blocking force, engaged it fiercely and drove it back over the demarcation line. In addition, the Beit Nuba National Guard moved up from the south to assist their neighbours and encountered a third ambush, which they engaged. The fact that the Israelis failed to get into the village, coupled with the initiative displayed by the Legion and National Guard junior commanders in their vigorous reaction to the attack, showed that at last the Legion was meeting with some success.

The most serious incident of this period, but one that was completely unlike the raids on frontier villages or police stations, took place in Jerusalem between 30 June and 2 July. It so chanced that the present writer was temporarily in command of the brigade on the Ramallah-Nablus front, with the 9th Regiment of which he was then Commanding Officer, in the Old City area. The Jerusalem Incident was a shooting match

Bedouins of the Desert Patrol during training at Amman, February 1943. (Imperial War Museum)

establishment—notably the provision of an urgently needed fourth infantry brigade. However, the Egyptian Government took the opportunity during the negotiations to foment a series of riots in the main Jordanian cities as part of Nasser's campaign to assert his leadership of the Arab world. These riots, in December 1955, taxed the loyalty and resources of the Legion to the utmost and it says much for the army that, with very few exceptions, they stood firm and carried out their unaccustomed internal security duties extremely well, despite the fact that they were involved in operations against their own countrymen.

Thus the internal tranquillity of Jordan was shattered. Sadly, she '. . . was to become just one more unstable, passionate, blood-stained Arab country'. Time was now fast running out for the Arab Legion. Although order was restored by January 1956, a personal campaign against Glubb Pasha was gathering momentum; a clique of younger officers had gained the ear of King Hussein and their efforts succeeded on 1 March 1956 when Glubb was summarily dismissed – so summarily in fact that he was required to leave the country, after thirty years in the service of Jordan, the next morning. Glubb was not unaware that the King, or rather his new friend Ali Abu Nawar, had been considering getting rid of him for some time. The immediate cause of his dismissal appears to have been the misinterpretation by the

which went on for three days, and caused a number of casualties, mostly civilians. The 9th Regiment had only one man wounded and that by the merest chance. On 3 July General Bennike, for the United Nations, thanked both sides for their co-operation in putting an end to the shooting, expressed his sympathy for the victims, and expressed a pious wish that the ceasefire would not be broken again. This satisfied nobody.

The Jordanians, considering that the Israelis had opened fire simultaneously all along the front, supposed that it was as the result of a prearranged plan. Nor was this wholly unreasonable since the Mixed Armistice Commission had recently condemned Israel for a raid on the village of Azzoun, a fact which fighting in Jerusalem could keep from the pages of the world Press. The Israelis for their part blamed the bedouin of the 9th Regiment, claiming that they were attempting to avenge their brethren in the 1st Regiment slain at Azzoun. This suggestion is simply untrue. The Regiment had only ten officers present at the time, and the senior officers, all lieutenants as it happened, were not capable of laying on such an operation without the knowledge and co-operation of their Colonel, which they neither had nor invited.

While the Legion had been getting to grips with the practical side of its task, the politicians had not been idle. Towards the end of 1955, Jordan had applied to join the Baghdad Pact, and negotiations took place in Amman which would have resulted in considerable increases to the Arab Legion's

On 13 March 1944 'Exercise Crocodile' took place in Palestine and Transjordan, directed by Lieutenant-General Holmes. Here, troopers of the Camel Corps on guard at the Director's camp are inspected by General Holmes. (Imperial War Museum)

King of an ammunition return, which seemed to show that stocks were dangerously low.

Be that as it may, Glubb departed, followed very shortly afterwards by the remainder of the sixty-four British officers at that time serving with the Legion. The existence of the Arab Legion, with its varied and distinguished history, may be said to have come to an end on that first day of March 1956, when a Jordanian radio announcer first referred to it officially as 'The Jordan Arab Army' – the title by which it has since been known.

The Leaders

KING ABDALLAH

Amir Abdallah originally arrived in Transjordan from the Hejaz in 1921, with the intention of raising a force of tribesmen for operations against the French in Syria. Winston Churchill, then the British Colonial Secretary, was in Cairo for the British Middle East Conference at that time and when he heard of Abdallah's arrival decided to meet him; it was as a result of this meeting that Abdallah was offered the Amirate of the country of which he later became king.

The new Amir was a very astute man, with a well-developed sense of humour; Kirkbride, for many years British Resident and later Ambassador in Amman, says of him '. . . he had a perennial twinkle in his eyes, which was an indication of his basic character'. At the same time, Abdallah was a man with considerable political experience, having spent much of his time as a young man in Constantinople among the ruling classes of the Ottoman Empire; Glubb comments that this early experience produced in him a 'wise and tolerant mind' – attributes which certainly stood the Amir in good stead in the trials to come and

enabled him to meet statesmen on their own ground.

Glubb also points out, however, that Abdallah was a very human man, with his faults like anyone else; he could be irritable, even vindictive to those he did not like and he was not always careful what he said – 'A man whose enemy is his own tongue' according to his cousin the Amir Shakir ibn Zeid. A sincerely religious man, at the height of the battle for Jerusalem in 1948 he told Glubb that he would rather die on the walls of the city than see the Jews in possession of the Holy Places.

As a ruler Abdallah was essentially a practical monarch, albeit with a romantic side, who put his country before all else. He alone amongst the Arab leaders could see the need for a genuine peace with the new state of Israel; after the 1949 Armistice he is quoted as saying: 'Israel is stronger than Jordan, therefore we cannot fight them. Israel wants peace. Why not see what they have to say? Perhaps we shall get better terms that way.' The King ignored the denunciations that poured in on him from the other Arab countries and eventually this was to prove his undoing when, in July 1951, he was murdered in the city he loved, Jerusalem.

That Jordan had been the peaceful and prosperous country it had for so many years was to a very large extent due to the wise leadership of King Abdallah; a statesman moreover who was prepared to stand by his country's friends, and who did not hesitate to declare war on Germany as England's ally in 1939. The grief felt throughout Jordan when Abdallah died was undoubtedly genuine; the people of Jordan had lost a king aptly described by Stewart Perowne as a 'great ruler, inflexible friend and most royal gentleman'.

KING HUSSEIN

Hussein, grandson of King Abdallah, was King of Jordan and Commander-in-Chief for the last three years of the Legion's existence, and his was the decision which brought about the end of the Legion as it had grown up under Peake and Glubb. Although the son of a devoted father, that father, King Tallal, had become insane; in addition the prince had been with his grandfather, Abdallah, when he was assassinated in 1951, hardly an

Amir Abdallah decorates a Legionnaire for valour shown during the Syrian campaign. (Imperial War Museum)

Hussein. Glubb says of the King that he is very like his grandfather, who was also impetuous in his youth, and expresses the opinion that if Hussein can maintain his throne into middle age he has every chance of becoming as great a man as Abdallah was. It is indeed certain that, since Glubb's departure, the King has shown himself to be a man of courage and initiative, having retained control in Jordan through countless crises, including an attempted *coup d'état*, a disastrous war with Israel and civil war against the various Palestine guerrillas – any one of which could easily have brought him down. If his judgment is sometimes suspect he seems to have luck on his side. Perhaps Glubb should have the last word – 'He is a man of character and courage, who may render great service to the Middle East if he survives these uncertain times.'

PEAKE PASHA (1886–1970)

Lieutenant-Colonel Frederick Gerard Peake, C.M.G., C.B.E., who created the Arab Legion and commanded it for seventeen years, had a conventional early career – public school, Sandhurst, and a regular commission in The Duke of Wellington's Regiment. Not content with peacetime soldiering in England, in 1906 he arranged to be posted to the second battalion of his regiment in India, but found the gay social life there equally unattractive, and in 1913 he obtained a secondment to the Egyptian Army. Peake saw no service on the main fronts in the First World War, although he did take part in the Darfur expedition

auspicious start for a young and inexperienced monarch. Hussein, after a period at school in Alexandria, completed his education in England at Harrow and then at the R.M.A. Sandhurst. When he returned for his coronation in 1953 his chief characteristic was an impeccable Brigade of Guards salute; there were those who described him, unkindly, as 'Made in England'. At that period the chief impression he gave was one of extreme shyness. He was at his most confident when handling a plane or a car.

In 1953 Jordan was already facing increasing activity on her frontier with Israel, and political attacks from other Arab states, Egypt in particular. Thus from the outset the pressures on the King were great and it is not surprising that in his enthusiasm for things military he listened, at least from 1955 onwards, to the voices of a small clique of ambitious young Arab officers, in preference to that of Glubb, a man thirty-eight years his senior and, moreover, a man who had advised his grandfather. Hussein's judgment seems to have been at fault in dismissing Glubb and the other British officers in the way he did, and yet it is understandable. In fact the men who brought about Glubb's dismissal were also out to dethrone

One of King Abdallah's personal bodyguard of Circassians

H.M. King Hussein, escorted by troopers of the Household Cavalry Squadron, inspects the Arab Legion at the Arab Legion Day Parade, 1955

in the Sudan in 1915. Disappointed at not seeing more active service, he made his way, whilst ostensibly on leave, to Salonika and spent some five months as an observer with the R.F.C. In April 1918 he joined the Egyptian Camel Corps and was sent to Feisal's Arab Army, operating on Allenby's eastern flank in Transjordan – the first view Peake had of the country he was to serve for so many years.

Peake earned a considerable reputation as a demolitions expert, so successful was he at sabotaging the Hejaz Railway. A photograph of him at this time shows us a fine-drawn, rather haggard, face, with a pointed beard already greying and with piercing, almost fanatical, eyes. It is not difficult to imagine him as the 'hot, impatient soul' described by T. E. Lawrence, nor as a 'twelfth-century Arab swashbuckler' – another contemporary description. This, then, was the man who was sent to Transjordan in 1920 to form the Arab Legion. However, he soon revealed different talents, those of an administrator, and although his courage and ability as a soldier are not in question, it is perhaps for these that he should be remembered. Peake's primary task, as he saw it, was to show the flag around the country; this was important as many of the country districts, particularly areas in the south such as Kerak and Tafileh, were without any representatives of law and order. One result of Peake's indefatigable tours was that he became the arbiter in numerous local disputes, frequently being asked to press the case with the Government in Amman for some local project such as a new road or irrigation

scheme; equally frequently he received the credit when these things were eventually provided.

Peake's tours were not always without excitement. On one occasion near Madaba he and his small escort came under fire from a nearby ridge, lined with the heads and rifles of the Beni Hemeida. Peake went forward alone and managed to identify himself, whereupon the tribesmen came rushing forward to greet him, apologizing profusely and protesting that they were merely protecting their homes and herds. While Peake was lunching with the sheikh after this encounter a party of merchants passed by along the track he had followed, and it became very clear why the Beni Hemeida were there. A meaning look from those piercing blue eyes showed the sheikh that Peake understood the situation, and such was the strength of his personality that the tribe gave little further trouble.

However, it was not until after the Anglo-Transjordan Treaty was signed in 1927 that Peake's abilities as an administrator really came to the fore; his first seven years in Transjordan had been spent almost exclusively in raising and training the Legion and in keeping the peace. He was determined to do more than this for the country and was anxious for the development of a prosperous and stable Arab government. With the more peaceful conditions then prevailing – at least until 1936 – Peake was able to turn his attention to less military pursuits. He saw, for instance, the benefits to the local population (and incidentally to the police) of refurbishing the old Roman road which ran from Aqaba to Amman over the highlands via Kerak, Tafileh and Shobek. A large part of this road was reconstructed during Peake's service and, although not metalled throughout its length until the late 1950s, it became a very adequate route for motor vehicles in all except the very worst weather. Peake also instigated the repair of part of the old Roman irrigation systems, in particular the underground reservoirs, with the result that, in the increasingly secure atmosphere, the villagers began to plant orchards and to till fields further away from the safety of their homes; there was such an increase in cultivation that in the late 1920s Transjordan, often dismissed as a desert country, was in a position to export grain to Palestine.

To Peake must go much of the credit for the remarkable stability of Transjordan at this time. His firm touch was felt everywhere; not only in the Legion, whose smartness and efficiency were a byword in the Middle East, but also in the civil administration of the country. Peake had early realized that only Arabs can really control Arabs and so, while keeping a close eye on general administration as he travelled about the country, and though little escaped him, he very rarely interfered.

Peake had captured the hearts, not only of the men of the Arab Legion, but of the country as a whole. The code-word 'Thundercloud' used to precede him on his visits, and he was capable of great anger, though whether real or assumed is uncertain. What is certain is that he was a man of great kindness and consideration for others. Glubb recounts how Arabs would often say of him, 'Peake Pasha – God bless him – his heart was simple.' A contemporary photograph, taken in the 1930s, shows a tall, erect and impressive figure in blue patrols, very much master of the situation, and perhaps more at ease with himself than the man portrayed ten years before.

Peake's departure from Transjordan in 1939 was almost a royal progress as he travelled south towards Aqaba. In Amman the Amir Abdallah called on him personally to say farewell. His impact on the people of Transjordan was demon-

strated by the way whole villages turned out to wish him well. At El Udrah the Howeitat under Hamd Ibn Jazi had assembled in force, while at Ma'an were drawn up all the tribes from the Wadi Sirhan and the Wadi Rum. Finally, just before Peake's car crossed into Sinai on its way to Port Said, his chief-of-staff, Abdel Kader, arrived by courtesy of the R.A.F., who had flown him down from Amman so that he could say a final farewell to Peake on the frontier line. There can be few foreigners who have inspired such universal liking in the country of their adoption. His published works include *The History and Tribes of Jordan*.

Peake's decorations included the Order of El Nahda (First Class); the Order of El Istiqlal (Second Class) and the Syrian order Pour le Mérite.

GLUBB PASHA:

Lieutenant-General Sir John Bagot Glubb, K.C.B., C.M.G., D.S.O., O.B.E., M.C.

Born in 1897 Major J. B. Glubb, O.B.E., M.C., came to Transjordan in 1930 and, like Peake, was no stranger to the Arab scene, although he had not arrived in the Middle East until after the First World War. Unlike Peake he had seen action, in the Royal Engineers from 1915 in France, where he was thrice wounded. One of his wounds left a permanent scar earning the nickname of *Abu Henaik – Henaik* meaning 'jaw' – among the bedouin, who love to bestow nicknames. In his own words 'the barrack square at Chatham was more than monotonous' and he leapt at the chance of a more adventurous life when, in 1920, volunteers were required for service in Iraq. While there Glubb became interested in the bedouin and their way of life and in 1924 spent his leave on a 500-mile journey by camel, in itself no mean achievement, across the Syrian desert from Iraq to Transjordan, being received by the Amir Abdallah on his arrival. However, it was to be another six years before Glubb, who had acquired some reputation for his success in bringing peace to the nomadic tribes of Iraq, was invited to do the same in Transjordan.

When Glubb entered the service of the Amir Abdallah he was already something of an expert in bedouin tribal laws and customs and was a

Colonel Frederick Gerard Peake feasting in a Bedouin tent with his staff officer and friend Abdul Qadir Bey Al Jundi in the late 1920s

Arab Legion trumpeter blowing: 'Assembly'. (Imperial War Museum)

When the man's brother arrived, threatening to shoot Glubb, the latter retaliated by rounding up all the tribe's camels and handing them over to a nearby detachment of the Transjordan Frontier Force. When later that same day the tribesmen rode up to Glubb's camp with apologies for the incident, Glubb returned the camels with an admonition not to neglect the vital piquet duty again. Glubb like Peake before him had early appreciated that the formal regulations of established government are not always the most appropriate answer to tribal problems. Glubb's original approach had not only prevented a nasty incident, it had taught an idle man a lesson (without the arrest and imprisonment he deserved and probably expected). *The people follow the strong man*, says an Arabic proverb. One need not suppose that this outburst of righteous rage did anything to lessen Glubb's prestige.

The Government had agreed to withdraw the troops from the desert and the enlistment of local men in the Desert Patrol was an essential part of Glubb's plan, but it was not until 1931 that the Howeitat began to join, having at last become convinced by Glubb's determination that if they did not he would enlist men from other tribes to police them.

The picture of Glubb that we have at this time is that of a man of almost unlimited energy, completely involved with the Arabs and in particular the bedouin. The fact that all tribal raiding had ceased by the middle of 1932 is a remarkable tribute to his courage, personality and energy, especially when it is remembered that he carried out the task with no more than ninety men, and with no bloodshed, fines or imprisonments.

Glubb continued to command in the desert until 1939, when Peake retired, and so was not directly concerned in the 1936 Palestine troubles, which did so much to poison relations between the Arab world and Great Britain. However, once Glubb assumed command of the Legion, he felt increasingly the pressure from the bedouin on one side and the settled Arabs on the other. Glubb became increasingly involved in the political life of Transjordan – one suspects with some reluctance – and although he got on well with the Amir Abdallah, relations with the Amir's ministers were not always so smooth. It seems likely that many of

fluent Arabic speaker. He was also an extremely patient man, which was fortunate because for some time after his arrival in Transjordan he was unable to persuade anyone to join the desert police force which he saw was needed to end the tribal raiding. Glubb spent the first few weeks touring the tents of the Howeitat, the tribe principally concerned in raiding – and being raided – across the Saudi-Transjordan border, trying to get himself accepted as someone who was anxious to help, rather than the representative of an unfeeling Government. Gradually Glubb began to gain the tribe's confidence and a plan to end the destructive raiding began to evolve; he managed to organize a system of tribal piquets who would warn the remainder of the tribe if a raiding party approached, and this meant that the Howeitat could continue to use their traditional grazing areas right up to the frontier. However, when Glubb detected one of the piquet commanders forty miles from his post, standing at the door of his tent, the quiet-voiced Englishman showed another side to his character. He struck the man.

Drum section of the Arab Legion Band, October 1944. There are three bands in the Legion, the blue, the red and the green. In winter they wear khaki battle-dress, and in the summer white service dress. They can be distinguished one from the other by the colour of their lanyards, epaulettes and pipes. All musicians wear a lyre badge on the right arm above the elbow. (Imperial War Museum)

Glubb is a deeply religious man, his thirty years in the service of a predominantly Muslim state giving him a rare insight into the relationship of that religion with Christianity. Nowhere is this more evident than in his masterly analysis of the Jewish-Arab problem, with its roots deep in the three great religions of the Middle East, revealed in his *Peace in the Holy Land*. He is also a philosopher. Glubb's eventual dismissal from the Arab Legion, if not entirely unexpected, was executed in a particularly abrupt manner. A lesser man would have been unable to conceal his resentment and yet Glubb, in his account written soon after the event, could say, without apparent bitterness, '. . . I should like . . . to acknowledge my gratitude to the Hashemite royal family . . . from whom I received innumerable kindnesses.' The contrast of Glubb's hurried departure by air at six o'clock in the morning with Peake's grand exit is a sad commentary on the decline in the affairs of Transjordan. Glubb for his part has always maintained that his dismissal was perfectly legal, his only regret being the manner of it and the fact that he had perforce lost contact with so many friends in Jordan.

In an earlier book I described him as 'engineer officer, arabist, tribal judge, author, minister and general, not one after the other, but simultaneously'. This may stand, but it says nothing of his humour and his courtesy, and the quiet way in which he managed to give in his peculiar voice the most unequivocal orders on a multitude of subjects. Some of his British officers thought his long years in Arab lands had made him as devious as an Arab. For my part I think he just understood the ways of the world.

COOKE PASHA

Born in 1903, Major-General Sidney Arthur Cooke, C.B., O.B.E., joined the Arab Legion in 1951 to assume command of 1 Division. Like many officers who came to the Legion, he was no stranger to Jordan, having some years previously commanded his battalion, the Royal Lincolns, when it had formed part of 'O' Force, the British Garrison in Aqaba.

A tall, broad-shouldered man, 'Sam' Cooke was always immaculately dressed and set a high

the latter suspected Glubb's motives and thought that, given the opportunity, he would have used his loyal bedouin soldiers to keep them in their place. That such a thought would never occur to a man of such unshakeable integrity as Glubb is apparent throughout his writings; his own concept of his duty as a servant of Transjordan and its King and Government comes over with complete sincerity.

19

standard for an already well-turned-out division. The particular attributes which he brought to the Legion were those of an organizer and administrator, and there is little doubt that the efficiency of 1 Division, probably at its peak about mid-1955, was largely the result of his efforts. He was possessed of great patience – an essential quality for any British officer with the Arab Legion. Arab soldiers are amongst the keenest to learn, but it must be admitted that they do not always take kindly to European discipline and the thorough training which most modern weapons require.

Patient though Cooke was, he could be caustic. Never hesitating to take a decision himself, he could be intolerant of others who were less decisive. On one occasion a staff officer, questioned as to the action taken over some incident, admitted that he had in fact done nothing. 'To do nothing', came the classic rejoinder, 'is always wrong'.

Cooke never had to command his division in full-scale operations but he was faced with the almost equally difficult task of training it for war, while simultaneously directing defensive operations on the West Bank under conditions not of peace but of armistice. Towards the end he had also to deal with a massive internal security problem in Amman and the main towns and refugee camps on the East Bank. These heavy responsibilities never affected his *sang froid*. After the assassination of King Abdallah, Glubb telephoned him orders for the maintenance of law and order in Jerusalem. 'One thing about Cooke was that he was always calm; he acknowledged his orders', Glubb wrote, 'as if I had said "Come round and have a drink".' A man, in short, who inspired confidence in all those under his command.

LASH BEY

Captain N. O. Lash, who had already had a four-year tour with the Legion, but who had been posted to a staff appointment in Palestine in 1938, rejoined in 1939, shortly before the start of the Second World War. He replaced Glubb as commander of the Desert Patrol, but this particular responsibility lasted only until 1941, when he went as Glubb's second-in-command with Habforce to Baghdad.

To Lash, leading an Arab Legion patrol across the frontier, fell the honour of the first skirmish of the Iraq campaign, when he brought in some tribesmen who had been on a reconnaissance for the Iraqi garrison in Rutbah. Lash took part in practically all the engagements leading to the capture of Baghdad, acquiring a reputation for coolness under fire. He then played a prominent part in the Syrian campaign, culminating in the action at Sukhna. He made himself slightly unpopular with the soldiers at Palmyra, when, with some difficulty, he restrained Sergeant Salim as Som'ari and his over-enthusiastic troop from trying to capture the town entirely on their own!

The rest of the war Lash spent as Glubb's assistant in the monumental task of creating a modern army out of what had been little more than a tribal police force. Thus it was that when the Arab Legion took the field again in 1948 it was Lash, now with the rank of brigadier, who commanded the division of two brigades which crossed the Jordan on 15 May. Lash bore the responsibility for the day-to-day tactical control of the Arab Legion throughout the 1948 fighting, a command which he exercised with ability and courage, leaving Glubb the overall control of the war and the unenviable task of dealing with the politicians.

No other Arab army achieved as much as the Arab Legion and the end of hostilities in 1949 found Jordan impoverished but the Legion itself victorious, having secured a considerable area of

Glubb Pasha, Commandant of the Arab Legion, seated (centre) with a group of Legion officers, 30 October 1944. (Imperial War Museum)

Palestine for the Arabs. Lash retired in 1951, and returned to England, in order to make way for a more experienced soldier at a time when the Legion was expanding. He could look back with pride on his service in Jordan.

The Infantry

When Peake first raised the Arab Legion in 1920 he saw it primarily as a force to protect the 'Sown' against the 'Desert'. It was clear to him that with the passing of Turkish authority, the bedouin were encroaching on the Arabs of the settled areas; unless this trend could be checked no stable Arab government would be formed in Transjordan. The original Arab Legion infantry were therefore deliberately recruited from the townsfolk and villagers – the *haderi*. It was not until 1936, when the Desert Mechanized Force was raised, that the bedouin were included in any numbers in the infantry, the new unit being recruited exclusively from the desert nomads.

The lorried infantry of the Desert Mechanized Regiment, as it later became, performed their function very well, although they were never organized on a proper battalion basis, consisting as the regiment did of a number of troops each of between fifty and seventy men. It was during the Second World War that infantry battalions on the British model began to be raised, 1st, 2nd and 3rd Regiments being the first to be grouped into a brigade, followed by another three regiments for a second brigade. It was these two brigades, plus a number of independent Guard Companies, which formed the infantry arm when the Arab Legion moved into Palestine in 1948. The Guard Companies were not fully-trained infantry soldiers, having been raised during the war for the sole purpose of guarding military camps and depôts

throughout the Middle East. That they had done this unglamorous job superlatively well did not make up for the fact that they possessed no machine-guns or other support weapons and had not, in most cases, had any more than the most rudimentary field training. They had not, of course, experienced practical offensive operations. All the more credit to them, therefore, that in the 1948 fighting they soon learnt, and learnt well, the infantryman's job.

After the Rhodes Armistice in 1949 came the rapid expansion of the Legion based on the establishment of a conventional British infantry division. Amalgamation of the Guard Companies, and new recruitment produced enough men to form nine battalions, numbered 1 to 9, and these were grouped into three brigades to form the basis of the new division; later the 10th, known sometimes as 'The Hashemite', Regiment was also raised. This extra battalion proved to be an invaluable, though small, reserve which allowed the divisional commander a little flexibility in deployment, so as to reconcile the operational commitments on the West Bank with the urgent need to train his expanding division. When 4th Armoured Brigade was formed it was proposed that one infantry battalion – 1st Regiment was provisionally earmarked for the task – should be trained in the armoured infantry rôle and should form the infantry element in the new armoured brigade; the general political situation prevented this happening before 1956, although some time

Pipers of the Legion on parade; they were trained to play the bagpipes by the pipers of the Black Watch. (Imperial War Museum)

after Glubb Pasha was dismissed 1st Regiment was eventually equipped with Saracen armoured personnel carriers.

Although both bedouin and *haderi* were now recruited for the infantry, it was never Legion policy to mix the two in the same battalion, so that 1st, 2nd, 3rd, 7th and 9th Regiments were all-bedouin battalions (except for a number of clerks, signallers, storemen, cooks and orderlies), while the remaining battalions were all-*haderi*; brigades were made up from battalions of either. The two types of soldier had very different characteristics, some good, some bad. The bedouin tribes vary one from another, but in general they are a feckless, volatile and cheerful people, but who are nevertheless very hardy, take well to soldiering and can accept discipline; however, they need to be led, not driven. The great military weakness of the bedouin soldier, at least in the early days, was his reluctance to take up a static defensive position. But if he needs some persuasion to dig in, he needs little to launch into an attack. This attitude explains the disobedience to orders at Sukhna in 1941, and at the same time accounts for the victory, for without the dash displayed on that occasion by the bedouin of the Mechanized Regiment, outnumbered as the Legion was, the outcome of the battle might have been very different. The bedouin produce excellent platoon and section commanders.

The Jordanian *haderi*, on the other hand, makes a solid and dependable infantryman who, if well

led, can hold his own with any Arab soldier. The officers tend to be better educated than the bedouin, but are politically minded and fond of their creature comforts. Like so many educated Arabs, they tend to think of academic qualifications as a passport to any position of authority, and Glubb tells of his difficulty in persuading Jordanian politicians that possession of a university degree does not of itself make a man officer material. This is not to say that there are not excellent *haderi* infantry officers.

Both bedouin and *haderi* proved extremely enthusiastic and keen to learn; experienced foreign soldiers visiting the Legion invariably retained a good impression of them, and Field-Marshal Templar for one, after inspecting the 9th Regiment in 1955, is on record as saying: 'Tell them that in time of war I would rather have them on my side than against me.'

The British element in the infantry was small, only four of the battalions, all bedouin, having British commanding officers; the three brigade commanders were also British, but only one had a British brigade-major and he was replaced by an Arab officer in 1954. Nevertheless, like the other arms, the infantry suffered from a lack of experienced senior Jordanian officers, though possibly less than most. For its first twenty years the Legion had been very largely restricted to police duties and even in the Second World War, through no fault of its own, its active participation in operations had been limited. This meant that by 1956, when the Legion's strength had risen to some 27,000 men, there was no Jordanian officer with proper military training more than 36 years old. This was of course, the main justification for the presence of the British officers in the senior command positions and, in the more technical units, at lower levels; but the rapid expansion also meant, Glubb always being very insistent on no promotion without proper qualification, that companies were often commanded by captains or lieutenants and platoons by cadets serving a qualifying period before finally receiving their commissions. It was not uncommon for platoons to be commanded by sergeants or even corporals. This situation was as true of the infantry as of the other arms and in most battalions the only major was the second-in-command. Sometimes the

Arab Legionnaires during infantry training at a recruits' depot, 1944. (Imperial War Museum)

22

Bedouins of the Desert Patrol Camelry. (Imperial War Museum)

second-in-command was a captain or even a lieutenant, but this was of no great importance.

By the mid-1950s battalion organization had been standardized on the British model, with some differences, and consisted of Battalion Headquarters, four rifle companies each of three platoons, a support company and a headquarters company. The basic sub-unit of the platoon was the section, of which there were three, each of nine men. The support company consisted of a mortar platoon, a machine-gun platoon, an anti-tank platoon and, eventually, an assault pioneer platoon; headquarter company included signal, transport and administrative platoons. The major differences between the Arab Legion and the British battalion concerned numbers and trans-

port. The Legion was a long-service volunteer army, where the average length of service of all ranks was about four and a half years; in general the difficulty was in turning men away, not in persuading them to join. This meant that whereas a British battalion in the 1950s had an establishment of about 750 men, invariably under-implemented, Arab Legion battalions were always well over 800 strong and sometimes exceeded 900 men. The second difference, transport, lay in the fact that the Arab Legion battalion had sufficient organic transport to lift the entire battalion, whereas in the British Army at that time a battalion had to call on the R.A.S.C. if it wished to move more than one company by road transport; otherwise it marched. Arab Legion battalions

23

Trials of the Legion's prototype anti-tank vehicle constructed from a Ford-Canadian three-ton truck. December 1953

were, in effect, lorried infantry, as indeed the old Mechanized Regiment had been in 1939, and this was an essential requirement when battalions had to be ready to reinforce the West Bank troops at very short notice. It also made the unit much more flexible for training, and was a tremendous asset in internal security operations.

Weapons allocation to the infantry followed in general the British pattern, the Mark III, then the No. 4, ·303 rifle being the basic platoon weapon coupled with the Bren light machine-gun and the Sten sub-machine-carbine for section commanders. 2-inch mortars were held in each platoon, while heavy support weapons consisted of the 3-inch mortar, Vickers medium machine-gun and the 6-pounder anti-tank gun. The 6-pounders were replaced in 1954 by the 17-pounder anti-tank gun, in order to give the battalion a better anti-tank capability. This decision followed current British Army thought and the infantry battalions were faced with the same problem as the British had been, that of finding a suitable gun tractor to tow this large and heavy weapon, and to carry an adequate supply of its bulky ammunition. The British solution had been to use a tracked carrier, but the Legion could not afford this and 3-ton trucks had to be employed, with all their attendant problems of concealment and vulnerability in the forward areas. An entirely different answer to the problem of anti-tank defence of the infantry battalion had been considered in 1953. The Legion possessed a large number of Ford Canadian 3-ton trucks, and a

design to mount the 17-pounder over the rear axle of this vehicle, with limited traverse over the rear arc, was evolved. The truck superstructure was entirely removed and side and limited overhead protection against shell fragments and small-arms fire was planned. The problem of vulnerability was thus to some extent overcome, and concealment too since the highest point on this unusual vehicle was the steering wheel. A prototype was built and performed very well on user trials in late 1953, but unfortunately the project, which had interesting possibilities, was not pursued and battalions were issued with their towed guns.

As in most armies, there were never enough infantry battalions to cope with all the Legion's tasks and because of this all regiments saw active service in one form or another between the years 1949 and 1956. Thus the Arab Legion infantry can fairly be said to have formed the mainstay of the army and to have been, in general, equipped and trained well up to modern standards.

The Royal Armoured Corps

The Arab Legion Royal Armoured Corps – a title bestowed on it by King Hussein in 1954 – may be said to have had its beginnings as long ago as 1939, when Glubb Pasha invested in six home-made armoured trucks mounting machine-guns only, manufactured, ironically enough, by the German-Jewish firm of Wagner in Jaffa. Fighting vehicles of a sort, in the shape of unarmoured trucks armed with Lewis guns, the Legion already had, and between them these two types of vehicle

Desert Patrol (Badieh)

MICHAEL ROFFE

A

1 Colonel (Qaimakam), 1955
2 Commander, Mounted Bodyguard, 1955
3 Major-General (Qaid el Firqa), 1955

MICHAEL ROFFE

1 **Lieutenant-Colonel (Qaid), 9th Infantry Regiment, 1955**
2 **Standard-Bearer, 7th Infantry Regiment, 1953**
3 **Colour-Sergeant (Naguib), 9th Infantry Regiment, 1954**

Trooper, Mounted Police (Fursan), 1955

D

1 Drummer, Arab Legion Band, c. 1953
2 Cadet, Cadet Training School, Amman, 1953
3 Drum-Major, Arab Legion Band, c. 1955

MICHAEL ROFFE

E

1 Corporal (Areef), Circassian Bodyguard,
  1955
2 Trooper, Jundi Than's Armoured Car
  Regiment, 1955
3 Trooper, Camel Corps, 1955

MICHAEL ROFFE

Trooper, Household Cavalry Squadron, 1955

1 Corporal (Areef), Arab Legion Engineers,
  c. 1954
2 Constable, Police, 1955
3 Private, National Guard (Haris el Watani),
  1954

H

rendered yeoman service to the Mechanized Force throughout the Iraq and Syrian campaigns of 1941, and indeed for many years after.

It was not until 1945 that the Legion acquired a more up-to-date armoured fighting vehicle, the Marmon-Herrington armoured car. These vehicles, which were South African built from British and United States components, had been extensively used in the Western Desert before being passed on to the Legion, but they were rugged and easily-maintained machines, well-suited to the technical capabilities of the Legion at that time. However, after a few years it was realized that the 2-pounder gun, which formed the main armament of the Marmon-Herrington, had limited range and penetration when matched against the current Israeli tanks. Colonel Broad-hurst, the Legion's Senior Technical Officer, devised an extension to the turret mantelet which would allow the 6-pounder anti-tank gun to be mounted instead; production of cars with this modification, carried out entirely in Arab Legion workshops, started in 1953 and eventually all armoured car squadrons had a proportion of these up-gunned vehicles.

The armoured cars had been incorporated within infantry battalions to start with, and were used effectively by them in the 1948 fighting. However, when the Legion began to reorganize into a conventional infantry division it was decided to concentrate the armour into one unit – 1st Armoured Car Regiment. This unit was organized on the lines of a British armoured car regiment, within the limitations of the equipment available, and consisted of Regimental Headquarters, three 'sabre' squadrons, a headquarters squadron, signals troop and Light Aid Detachment. The basic sub-unit was the reconnaissance troop; in the British service at that time this would have been made up of two armoured cars and two scout cars. No scout cars were available in the Legion, so Landrovers were used instead and these vehicles (the original 80-inch short wheelbase version) were suitably modified to carry two men only, a radio plus spare batteries and a forward-firing Bren light machine-gun. No canopies or windscreens were fitted and the rear of the vehicle was built up to carry the crew's kit, spare petrol, etc. In addition to the reconnaissance troops, each squadron

A visit by H.M. King Hussein to the Divisional Regiment, Arab Legion Royal Armoured Corps, November 1954

had a support troop consisting of five sections of assault troopers and three 3-inch howitzers. No suitable armoured personnel carriers were available and either 1-ton trucks or armoured cars with the turrets removed were used in the support troops; similar turretless armoured cars provided the howitzers with a self-propelled mount.

Once 1st Armoured Car Regiment was established, 2nd Armoured Car Regiment, similarly organized, began to form. Money was scarce and it was some time before the regiment could be brought up to establishment – in fact 2nd Armoured Car Regiment was never so lavishly equipped as 1st. The two regiments bore different distinguishing badges on their vehicles – the 1st being marked by crossed lances with pennants, while the 2nd adopted a hawk as its badge. The 2nd took, on the strength, a particularly fine specimen as its regimental mascot and it had its perch outside the commanding officer's office, where it proved somewhat disconcerting to the unwary visitor; the bird was carried on all formal parades and was trained to rear up and stretch its wings as the Landrover which carried it passed the saluting base. These two armoured car regiments were almost entirely bedouin-recruited, except for some of the attached personnel – signallers and fitters – and they each had only one British officer, the commanding officer; the British training captain, originally on the strength of 1st Armoured Car Regiment, was not replaced when his tour ended in 1953. All three of their British C.O.s afterwards became major-generals in the British Army.

In 1952 a small armoured headquarters was formed, later to become the headquarters of the 4th Armoured Brigade, when it was decided to add a tank regiment to the Legion's armoured forces. The British subsidy, which supported the Legion financially, was not large enough to pay for a complete armoured regiment on the British model and the only vehicle which the British were prepared to release at that time was the Valentine 17-pounder self-propelled gun, known as the Archer. While this armoured vehicle provided the anti-armour hitting power the Legion so badly needed – it outclassed any vehicle-mounted weapon the Israelis then had – it could in no sense be called a tank, since it had no overhead armour and the gun was restricted to firing over the rear arc of the vehicle. In the Legion, therefore, the Archer was used in the only feasible way – organized into a Divisional Regiment Royal Armoured Corps, the current British solution to the anti-tank defence of the infantry division. This *haderi*-recruited regiment was first called, somewhat unglamorously, The Divisional Regiment, but it later became the 3rd Tank Regiment and adopted a scorpion as its badge. The regiment consisted of a Regimental Headquarters, three 'sabre' squadrons each of twelve Archers, a headquarters squadron, signal troop and Light Aid Detachment; the basic sub-unit was the troop, made up of three Archers, the squadrons being commanded from Landrovers.

The Archers were shipped in four at a time

The colour party of the 2nd Armoured Car Regiment, with three of their Marmon-Herrington Mark IV armoured cars. The hawk is the regimental mascot

MARMON-HERRINGTON ARMOURED CAR, MK. IV
Technical Specifications
Crew: three – Commander/Loader, Gunner/Radio Operator, Driver. Weight: 6·5 tons. Length: 18 ft. 1·5 in. (wheelbase 9 ft. 10 in.). Width: 7 ft. Height: 7 ft. 6 in. Speed: 50 m.p.h. Engine: 95 b.h.p. Ford V8. Armament: Main – 2-pounder Quick-Firing anti-tank gun. Secondary – ·30 Browning coaxial machine-gun, ·30 Browning machine-gun in anti-aircraft mounting. Frontal armour: 12 mm. maximum. Radius of action: 200 miles

through the port of Aqaba, and thence by tank transporter to railhead at Ras al Naqb and by rail to Zerka – a journey not without its hazards on the narrow-gauge Hashemite Railway. (It was this railway, the Hejaz, which had so often been the target of T. E. Lawrence when Jordan was part of the Turkish Empire.) The operation continued slowly throughout 1953, but before the regiment could be completed to establishment, the British were persuaded that the Legion deserved something more up-to-date. In the early 1950s the Russian threat to Europe had accentuated the shortage of tank guns in the Western armies and in an effort to get more 20-pounder guns – then the main armament of the Centurion tank – into the hands of the troops, a design to up-gun the Cromwell

tank, of which large numbers were available, had been developed; the modified vehicle was called the Charioteer. Although Charioteer had all-round traverse and a fully-enclosed turret, its armour was thin and it was only really suitable as a tank-destroyer. In addition it suffered the grave defect of being unable to take up a fire position on a reverse slope if the ground in front fell away at all steeply; because the recoil of the 20-pounder could not be accommodated within the diameter of the Cromwell turret ring the gun had to be mounted high in the turret, allowing a correspondingly small angle through which the gun could be depressed. Indeed, so limited was the room inside the turret that the empty 20-pounder cases had to be ejected through a trap-door to the

CHARIOTEER
Technical Specifications
Crew: four – Commander, Gunner, Loader/Radio Operator, Driver. Weight: 28·5 tons. Length: 29 ft. (gun forward). Width: 10 ft. Height: 8 ft. 3 in. Track width: 1 ft. 3 in. Speed: 30 m.p.h. Vertical step: 3 ft. Engine: 600 b.h.p. Rolls Royce Meteor. Armament: Main – 20-pounder Quick-Firing tank gun. Secondary – ·30 Browning coaxial machine-gun. Frontal armour: 57 mm. maximum. Radius of action: 150 miles

**VALENTINE 17-POUNDER SELF-PROPELLED GUN
(ARCHER) (Imperial War Museum)**
Technical Specifications
Crew: four – Commander, Gunner, Loader/Radio
Operator, Driver. Weight: 16 tons. Length: 21 ft. 8 in.
Width: 9 ft. Height: 7 ft. 4 in. Track width: 1 ft. 2½ in.
Speed: 20 m.p.h. Vertical step: 2 ft. 6 in. Engine: General
Motors 6-cylinder two-stroke Diesel. Armament: 17-
pounder quick-firing anti-tank gun. Frontal armour:
65 mm. maximum. Radius of action: 90 miles

rear, and the designers had provided accommoda-
tion for a two-man turret crew only.

In 1954 the British agreed to release a number
of Charioteers to the Arab Legion and, despite
their disadvantages, they were seized on eagerly.
Eventually 3rd Tank Regiment was equipped
with two squadrons of Charioteers and one of
Archers, the surplus Archers being turned over to
the National Guard. 3rd Tank Regiment wasted
no time in installing a third man, as tank commander, in the turret of their new tanks and,
although the regiment was still committed officially
to the divisional anti-tank rôle, training in the
two Charioteer squadrons soon took on a dis-
tinctly armoured regiment flavour in which the
offensive rather than the defensive spirit pre-
dominated.

It had been recognized when the formation of a
tank regiment was first planned that the acqui-
sition of tracked vehicles would be a new departure

for the Legion and that they would introduce
entirely new problems. Accordingly an armoured
workshop was created to provide technical backing
for the new regiment, and incidentally for the rest
of the armoured units as well, and a few tank
transporters were obtained. In addition, the regiment was allowed a very high proportion of
British officers – the commanding officer, three
squadron leaders (later cut to two), a technical
adjutant and a warrant officer as technical quarter-
master-sergeant. This was unusual for the Legion,
where, if anyone, the commanding officer was the
only Briton and where squadrons were usually
commanded by captains or lieutenants and troops
or platoons often by cadets. However, the arrangement proved very worthwhile, the regiment
becoming operational by mid-1955 – a remarkably
short time considering that few of the soldiers had
even seen a tank before 1952.

One other operational unit formed part of the

Arab Legion Royal Armoured Corps and this was the Desert Reconnaissance Squadron. The squadron was entirely bedouin manned and commanded and had no British element. Equipped with Landrovers mounting ·50 calibre and ·30 calibre Browning machine-guns, this small force was trained for long range penetration behind enemy lines and for Special Air Service type raiding operations.

Finally there was the Armoured Corps Boys Squadron, which was formed in 1955 under the command of a British major. As the equipment of the armoured units became more sophisticated the problem of training the soldiers in its use became increasingly acute, and the Boys Squadron was formed in order to give the young entry a better start when they subsequently joined their regiments. Even in the comparatively well-established armoured car regiments unexpected training problems arose, a typical case being that of map-reading. The chief rôle of the armoured cars was of course reconnaissance, and the bedouin soldiers who formed the regiments had no difficulty whatever in finding their way about the desert; the problem arose when they were required to pass information back to headquarters. Car commanders often found great difficulty in relating their position on the ground to the map and experienced and otherwise most competent officers were frequently unable to give a correct grid reference or compass bearing.

Despite all these problems the soldiers in the armoured corps units mastered their equipment

Collar badge, 3rd Tank Regiment

remarkably well and made up with enthusiasm what they lacked in experience of armoured warfare. The 3rd Tank Regiment was not committed to action before 1956, except in a dismounted internal security rôle, but the armoured car regiments and the Desert Reconnaissance Squadron did a tour of frontier duty on the West Bank in 1955, in order to relieve the pressure on the infantry brigades, and displayed there a high order of operational efficiency.

Supporting Arms and Services

ARAB LEGION ROYAL ARTILLERY

At the very outset the Arab Legion had included an artillery element when, in 1921, two mountain guns were added to the force; this small artillery troop took part in the ill-fated El Kura expedition later that year, which resulted in the temporary disbandment of the Legion. Peake having re-formed the Legion, however, the guns proved their worth in his successful operation in May 1922, when a fortunate direct hit on the house of the headman at Tibna precipitated the surrender of the Kura tribesmen. From then until 1927 the guns, although no doubt in use from time to time, do not seem to have played any very prominent part in the Legion's operations, and in that year, with the arrival of the Transjordan Frontier Force, the Legion establishment was reduced. The Legion's rôle being now very largely that of a police force, there was no requirement for artillery and this arm was disbanded.

From 1927 to 1948 the Arab Legion was without its own artillery, even during the Iraq and Syrian campaigns of 1941 when artillery support would have been invaluable. Even in the expansion of the Legion towards the end of the Second World War no artillery was provided for the mechanized brigade then formed, and it was not until 1948 that eight 25-pounder guns were received. These were formed into two batteries each of four guns, to support the two infantry brigades which then existed. The battery commanders were British officers and there was one British warrant officer who was an Assistant Instructor in Gunnery. Thus the Arab Legion entered the fierce fighting in Palestine in 1948 with an almost total lack of experience in modern artillery techniques and with very little equipment; indeed the only officers who were capable of directing fire were the three Britons. Worse: only first line stocks of ammunition were held. However, despite these problems the guns proved to be invaluable and, by dint of extraordinary exertions on the part of battery commanders and individual gun detachments, coupled with extreme economy in expenditure of ammunition, were used to good effect.

In 1949 the reorganization of the Legion into a

Four of 'Glubb's girls' – the nickname given to bedouins serving with the Legion – of the Desert Patrol at field gun practice. (Imperial War Museum)

conventional infantry division also involved a considerable expansion of the artillery, the normal allocation to a division being three field regiments, consisting of three-, six- or eight-gun batteries, to support each infantry brigade. Shortage of money for equipment, and the technical training needed to raise three field artillery regiments imposed some delay on the expansion and it was not until 1954 that the third regiment was in being. Each regiment (numbered 1 to 3) was equipped with the 25-pounder field gun, long in service with the British Army, towed with its limber by a 3-ton truck; regiments also included British commanding officers and each had a British training major, all seconded from the Royal Artillery. Training was carried out in a very thorough manner and in the best traditions of the Royal Regiment. The result was most impressive; guns and vehicles were maintained in immaculate condition and to see a battery of the Arab Legion Royal Artillery coming into action was a demonstration of professional efficiency second to none. Annual practice camps were held, as in British service, and at these regiments were able to demonstrate on the open range the results of their year's training, under the critical eye of the Commander Arab Legion Royal Artillery.

The brigadier who commanded the artillery had a small headquarters of his own forming part of Headquarters 1 Division, so that he was readily available to advise the divisional commander on artillery matters. In addition to the field regiments, which formed the bulk of the Legion's artillery, he had two other units under his command, a combined anti-tank and light anti-aircraft regiment (4th Regiment) and the School of Artillery. In 1954 the 17-pounder anti-tank guns of the combined regiment were dispersed amongst the infantry battalion anti-tank platoons. This decision conformed to current British Army doctrine, which had led to the artillery handing over its anti-tank rôle to the Royal Armoured Corps, the formation of the 3rd Tank Regiment allowing the Arab Legion to do the same.

Air defence, now provided by 4th Light Anti-Aircraft Regiment equipped with the Bofors 40 mm. gun, was becoming of increasing importance in view of the continued increase in Israeli air power; particularly when it is remembered that at this time Jordan had no combat aircraft of her own. However, it must be admitted that the effectiveness of this regiment was bound to be limited since it was never, before 1956, equipped with radar and the other necessary fire direction equipment essential for the successful engagement of low-flying, high-speed aircraft.

Finally there was the School of Artillery, commanded by a British major, assisted by a British warrant officer. Courses on all aspects of gunnery were run by them and their Jordanian instructors for artillery officers and N.C.O.s, achieving a very high standard with slender resources. Almost all the Arab Legion artillery officers passed through this school, which had an influence out of all proportion to its size. Its success was largely due to the late Lieutenant-Colonel Shaun Richmond, M.C., R.A. (a major when he commanded the school), who was a brilliant arabist and an officer of first rate professional attainments.

ARAB LEGION ROYAL ENGINEERS

There had been no tradition of military engineering in the Legion before 1949, but the need for this arm of the service, as of so much else, became only too apparent as the army expanded. By 1951 a field engineer squadron, British commanded, was in existence and plans for expansion into an engineer regiment were in hand. Some of the Jordanian officers then in the engineers had had some technical training in Great Britain, but there was no pool of experienced officers on which to draw for any expansion.

In view of the technical nature of engineer work, and because the squadron was in much demand for actual engineering tasks, it was decided to form a separate training wing, initially under a British captain; later the wing was expanded into a training squadron, commanded by a major whose staff included two British warrant officers. As many young Jordanian engineer officers as possible were sent to the School of Military Engineering at Chatham for technical training and this did much to raise the standard; however, the majority of all ranks had to learn their trade with the limited resources available in Jordan.

At first field squadrons were permanently

English officer of the Arab Legion taking coffee in the soldiers' guest tent, October 1944. (Imperial War Museum)

allocated on formation to infantry brigades, but they tended to be misemployed and their training could not be properly supervised. In 1952 all engineer units were concentrated at Zerka, where a proper camp was built and the sappers were able to train as a regiment consisting of three field squadrons, a field park squadron, signals troop and Light Aid Detachment. The heavy equipment used by a modern engineer regiment was in very short supply and much had to be borrowed from the British Army in Egypt; nevertheless, by mid-1953 the Divisional Engineer Regiment was well-established, together with much of its heavy plant such as bulldozers and graders.

The training facilities at the Zerka camp eventually became very comprehensive and included small arms ranges, a driver training area, signal training facilities, trade training workshops and various tactical training facilities covering demolitions, mine laying and clearing and bridging. For more comprehensive bridging training, special camps were held from time to time in the Jordan valley.

The full concentration of the engineers as a regiment was, however, comparatively short-lived; as the number of engineer tasks in support of operations on the West Bank increased, the engineers found that they always had at least one field squadron deployed in the frontier areas, busily engaged in laying minefields, constructing airstrips for light aircraft and advising on defence works. This intense activity underlined the need for more engineer backing and a Base Engineer Regiment was formed to support the divisional engineers. This organization, which later became the Base Engineer Group, not only provided more elaborate workshop and plant facilities than the Divisional Engineer Regiment had at its disposal, but also included the Training Squadron, and a newly-formed Boys Squadron for the education of boys below military age who aspired to a place in the engineers.

The expanded Arab Legion Royal Engineers, the personnel of which were *haderi*, had a comparatively high British element compared with other arms, including a lieutenant-colonel, two majors and two warrant officers. Due to the overall shortage of experienced Jordanian officers throughout the Legion, particularly in the technical arms, the remaining appointments were filled by very junior officers indeed, in some cases by cadets with only one or two years service. Nevertheless the engineers performed their tasks remarkably well under the circumstances, and by 1956 could be compared very favourably with their British counterparts.

ARAB LEGION SIGNALS

Like the artillery, the Arab Legion Signals could trace their history back to the early 1920s and, as with the gunners, they suffered a temporary eclipse in 1927 when the strength of the Legion was cut. But it was soon evident that communications were important, even in a police force, and in fact radio was in almost constant use in the Legion for most of its history. However, it was not until the reorganization and expansion stemming from the Second World War that a proper signals organization was set up. Overall command was exercised by the Chief Signals Officer, a British lieutenant-colonel, whose own headquarters formed part of Arab Legion Headquarters in Amman. Directly under him came the Base Signals organization, most of which was at Zerka and which, incidentally, maintained an efficient and regular radio link with the Arab Legion Liaison Office in London. The Chief Signals Officer also maintained technical control of the Divisional Signal Regiment, which provided signals troops permanently attached to most major units and headquarters throughout 1 Division.

The standard achieved by the Arab Legion Signals was extremely high. It might reasonably be supposed that to man and maintain such a highly technical arm of the service would have presented a serious problem for a comparatively unsophisticated and, by European standards, uneducated people; in fact the reverse was true, no doubt in part because of the long experience within the Legion of radio and telephone. Not only was the standard of operating high, but radio repairs were also efficiently carried out in the Signals' own workshops. The equipment in general use at unit level was the No. 19 or No. 62 HF radio, both then becoming obsolescent in the British Army; in addition every desert fort manned by the Desert Patrol also had its No. 19 set. These radios were habitually worked over very long distances, both by voice and key, and it was rare that a Legion operator failed to get through. One of their more impressive techniques was their ability to transmit and receive morse messages without understanding a word of English, morse not lending itself to transliteration into Arabic. The most complicated message would be written out perfectly and handed to its recipient although the operator often had not the faintest idea as to its meaning.

In 1955 the newly-formed Arab Legion Air Support Signals Section, equipped with the latest ground-to-air communications, took the field for the first time and was used most effectively to direct ground attack exercises by the R.A.F. in support of Arab Legion ground forces; this was ample proof, if any were needed, of the Signals' claim to a standard of performance as good as, and perhaps in some cases better than, any to be found in the British Army.

ARAB LEGION ELECTRICAL AND MECHANICAL ENGINEERS

Vehicle repair facilities in the Arab Legion were, up until 1949, of a very rudimentary nature. However, as the technical arms gradually built up it became imperative to build up with them the necessary technical stores and workshops. For administrative convenience the Legion departed from normal British Army practice in that technical stores such as vehicle and weapon spares were grouped with the workshops under the Senior Technical Officer; a British lieutenant-colonel, under the Senior Technical Officer's direction, had his own headquarters within Headquarters 1 Division and had under his operational command the three infantry brigade and one armoured brigade workshops within the division. This arrangement took some time to implement and it was not until mid-1954 that all four workshops were in operation, one only – 4th Armoured Workshops – being British-commanded.

In addition to the divisional workshops, the Senior Technical Officer controlled two static workshops – a small one in Amman dealing with the staff cars and police vehicles based there, and a large base workshops at Zerka. Zerka Workshops, commanded by a British lieutenant-colonel, with a number of British warrant officers on his staff, had belonged to the Transjordan Frontier Force. Handed over to the Legion when the Frontier Force disbanded in 1948, by 1952 the workshops had expanded into an extremely well-equipped establishment, which could tackle repairs to all vehicles and guns, including tanks. There was a good instrument shop where optical equipment such as sights and binoculars could be repaired, and fabrication of complete assemblies and comprehensive overhaul of vehicles could be carried out; the up-gunning of the Marmon-Herrington armoured car, referred to in an earlier chapter, was undertaken in Zerka Workshops and the prototype 17-pounder, self-propelled anti-tank gun for the infantry was also built there.

Finally, training of young soldiers entering the Arab Legion Electrical and Mechanical Engineers

was not neglected, apprentice tradesmen being taught their basic skills in a special training centre forming part of Zerka Workshops.

Air, Sea, Police, National Guard and Training

ARAB LEGION AIR FORCE

The Arab Legion Air Force, which existed under that name until 1956 (shortly afterwards it became the Royal Jordanian Air Force) had no combat aircraft, although towards the end of 1955 pilots were beginning to be trained on Vampire jet fighters; combat aircraft did not arrive until some time after Glubb's dismissal. As late as 1950, when King Abdallah visited Aqaba to inspect the British garrison stationed there, he had perforce to travel in an Anson provided by R.A.F. Amman.

However, the King was most anxious to establish an air force and gradually aircraft were acquired and pilots trained; the air force was

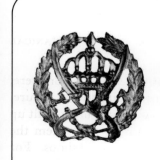

Regimental badges. Left: collar badge, staff officers only; centre: epaulette badge, as worn by all ranks and bearing the words 'Al Jeish al Arabi'; right: collar badge, infantry officers only

commanded by a British wing-commander, whose staff included a British squadron-leader, work-shops officer and technical warrant officers. By 1954 the Air Force could boast a communications flight of two de Havilland Doves, a Viking and a Monarch; unhappily the last-named crashed at Kolundia airport near Jerusalem soon after it had been received.

The next step for the Arab Legion Air Force was the formation of an air observation flight, whose primary task was to direct the fire of the army's guns. At that time this task in the British Army was carried out by officers in the Royal Artillery trained as pilots and flying Auster light aircraft; accordingly an officer was brought over to Jordan from the British troops in the Canal Zone of Egypt to train the Jordanians in the necessary techniques. Progress was slow but in time several qualified pilots took their place in the flight, and appeared for the first time in public in a fly-past at the 1955 Arab Legion Day Parade. The air observation flight in fact obtained little experience at directing the guns except during practice camps, but the Austers proved invaluable as communications aircraft, and carried out useful reconnaissance tasks during the cordon and search operations which took place in various parts of Jordan during the disturbances in early 1956.

ARAB LEGION FLOTILLA

Jordan has an outlet to the sea at the port of Aqaba, but it was not considered necessary for her to have any naval craft operating in the Gulf of Aqaba. However, after the 1948 fighting the truce line ran through the southern end of the Dead Sea,

Collar badge, Dead Sea Fleet

34

and accordingly steps were taken to find craft to patrol these salty waters. A motley collection were gathered together, typical of which were one or two infantry assault landing craft, on which 2-pounder guns in their turrets were mounted – removed from otherwise unserviceable Marmon-Herrington armoured cars. The Flotilla's craft also mounted Bren guns and some Browning machine-guns. These few craft patrolled the Dead Sea until, in 1955, the first of two high-speed launches arrived from Britain. These craft, which had been specially designed for operations in the Dead Sea – their hulls and metal fittings had been specially treated to resist the corrosive effects of the salt water – had to be brought overland from Aqaba – in itself no mean feat. They were armed with heavy and light machine-guns and the arrival of the first vessel gave the 'Dead Sea Fleet', as the Flotilla was popularly known, its first really effective craft for patrolling Jordanian waters.

Operating any boat on the Dead Sea was not only hard on the craft but could also be extremely unpleasant for the crew; the salt spray thrown up could be excruciatingly painful in any open cut, and after only a short exposure crews would come in covered with a thick layer of salt left behind by the evaporated water which had dried on them. Nevertheless the Jordanian crews took to the sea well enough, although one is quoted as saying, during a rough passage, 'I love the sea, were it not for the waves.' It was probably the physical difficulties, as much as any other factor, which prevented another product of the Senior Technical Officer's fertile brain from getting beyond the prototype stage. In order to give the Flotilla greater hitting power, his idea was to mount a 25-pounder gun on a simple catamaran hull powered by twin Ford V8 engines; although a perfectly practical proposition it would have been almost impossible to have protected the gun from serious corrosion, and the freeboard was so small that in anything but the calmest sea the crew would have found the conditions quite intolerable. However, with such resources as it had the Arab Legion Flotilla under its ex-Royal Marine com-mander (who inevitably became the 'Dead Sea Lord') maintained a Jordanian presence on the Dead Sea and was able to keep a close watch on such Israeli activity as there was in that area.

POLICE

Under Peake's original plan the police were formed into two distinct branches, the town police, in their familiar spiked helmets, who were on occasion used as infantry in the very early days, and the police cavalry, or mounted gendarmerie, who patrolled the country districts on horseback. The Desert Patrol, not formed until Glubb's arrival in 1930, were then added to the police force and they were generally camel-mounted, though from the earliest years of the Legion both they and the foot police had a proportion of motor transport; all police were armed with pistols, the mounted men carrying rifles in addition. These three basic divisions of the police force remained as the Arab Legion expanded, and Police Headquarters in Amman remained under the overall control of Arab Legion Headquarters, even though the police were entirely divorced from military operations after the formation of the first Arab Legion brigade during the Second World War. This combined command of military and police forces was of course contrary to all European practice, but in Jordan it worked extremely well.

In the country districts the police cavalrymen were required to carry out their duties very largely single-handed and with little supervision; this they did with such success that they acquired an authority which, in the eyes of the average villager, rated rather higher than that of the District Governor. In the towns the foot police established what must have been a unique record for Middle Eastern countries in that, for some thirty-four years up until the riots of October 1954, it had never been found necessary for the police to fire on a civilian crowd, so quiet and stable had the country been. In the desert, the main task of the *Badieh* – once they had put an end to tribal raiding in the early 1930s – was having routine patrols based on the stone police posts which were established throughout the desert areas. Such was the status of the Desert Patrol amongst the bedouin tribes, that at each fort a small patrol of a few men under an N.C.O. was effectively responsible for an area of many hundreds of square miles, their only contact with higher authority being the fort's radio working to Police Headquarters.

A troop of Mounted Police setting out on patrol, October 1944. An integral part of the Legion, the Police force consists of cavalry and infantry for the settled areas, and camelry for the desert. (Imperial War Museum)

It is perhaps the greatest testimony to the Arab Legion police to say that, up until 1956 at least, a traveller in Jordan was as safe as he would be in the English countryside and that tourists could, and frequently did, travel on their own anywhere in the country without the slightest difficulty.

NATIONAL GUARD

After the 1948 fighting King Abdallah granted Jordanian citizenship to every Palestinian refugee, and also to those still living in their homes on the West Bank in the area retained by Jordan after the Armistice. The Arab Legion was left with a frontier 400 miles long to guard and Glubb quickly saw that if the Legion was tied down in static defences its essential mobility would be destroyed. He therefore conceived the idea of forming an unpaid National Guard from the frontier villagers themselves, leaving the bulk of the Legion free to form a mobile reserve. At first his idea was received with scepticism by the politicians, who thought nobody would join – 'Fellaheen live for money . . . No money, no soldiers' summed up their attitude.

However, despite the gloomy forecasts Glubb went ahead with his plans, although there was little money available to pay for the minimum number of weapons required. Initially the National Guard consisted only of a few men in the frontier villages, but after the Government had been persuaded to pass a bill, making a month's annual National Guard training compulsory for all male

Jordanians of military age, the force quickly grew and eventually reached a strength of some 30,000 men.

National Guard regiments, who had little beyond their rifles and a limited number of Bren guns, were organized from groups of six to eight villages in an area; detachments garrisoned their own villages and did what they could to put them into a satisfactory state of defence with the few stores available – often little more than barbed wire. Arab Legion Headquarters retained a firm control over the National Guard and each detachment was under the command of a regular N.C.O., while the defence plans of regular units on West Bank duty were integrated, as far as possible, with those of the local National Guard Regiment. By 1956 training camps were set up in East Jordan so that proper courses could be run by the regular army for National Guardsmen – who received two pounds a month when away from home on training courses. At the same time equipment was gradually improving and the National Guard was well on the way towards becoming not

Men of the Desert Patrol on the march through the desert. In the background is a fort built in the thirteenth century and used by the kings of Damascus. (Imperial War Museum)

only a useful frontier defence force but also a worthwhile reserve for the Legion itself.

The setting up of the National Guard took time, and had to be on a strictly 'no cost' basis, whatever funds that could be scraped together being spent on weapons. However, the operational need existed from the start, with the result that in the early days the National Guard inevitably met some disastrous reverses, the Qibya incident in 1953 being one of the more spectacular. Nevertheless, many individual detachments did well against vastly superior and better trained forces, and at Beit Liqya in 1954, described in an earlier chapter, they put up a very creditable performance. Individual National Guard companies were also used, with some success, in support of regular troops on internal security duties in the Jordan valley in early 1956, thus giving the lie to those politicians who had said that if anyone joined the National Guard, which they thought unlikely, those that did would rise against the Government as soon as they had rifles in their hands. Nothing of the sort had happened and in fact the raising of the National Guard probably did more to raise the morale of the frontier villages, and to convince them that the Government in Amman had their interests at heart, than any other factor.

TRAINING ESTABLISHMENTS

Each arm of the Arab Legion was responsible for the specialist training of its own soldiers, in many cases, such as the engineers and artillery, setting up its own training centres and boys' schools for the purpose. In addition, however, there was a central training establishment, known as the Arab Legion Training Centre, at Abdali on the outskirts of Amman, which was responsible for initial recruit training, officer cadet training and some continuation training for N.C.O.s and officers.

All recruits entering the Legion had to pass through the Training Centre after enlistment and there they did a basic course of drill, weapon training and similar military subjects; a fairly large proportion of recruits were illiterate and these also received some primary education, although by 1955 many recruits came from the Legion's own schools and so illiteracy was not the problem it had been in the early days. The Training Centre

Bedouin cavalry recruits at drill on the parade ground of the Arab Legion Training Centre at Abdali. (Imperial War Museum)

was run by a British colonel, ably assisted by a warrant officer drill instructor from the Brigade of Guards, and these were the only British members of the staff; the training was rigorous and demanding and the smartness and bearing of Arab Legion soldiers was ample evidence of its effectiveness.

The officer cadet school, which formed part of the Training Centre, existed to train suitable candidates for commissions. Candidates were taken both from the ranks of the army in the shape of suitably qualified N.C.O.s, and also from civilian life; after a tough course candidates went to their regiments, still as cadets, to serve a preliminary period as troop or platoon commanders before finally being gazetted second-lieutenant.

The Training Centre's third main responsibility, that of continuation training for N.C.O.s and officers, consisted largely of advanced drill and weapon training courses for the former and company and equivalent commanders' tactical courses for the latter. The Arab Legion had a careful selection and qualification system for promotion, and this higher level training assisted N.C.O.s and officers to qualify.

Officers' staff training presented the Legion with another problem entirely. The Legion had to rely heavily on the British element for its senior staff officers, simply because it had few suitably trained officers of its own to fill the posts created at various headquarters as the army expanded. Glubb managed to persuade the British to reserve two places a year at the Staff College, Camberley for Jordanian officers, but the political pressure on him to replace the British officers in the Legion by Jordanians was continually growing; so it was that in early 1955 the Arab Legion's own Staff College was created and was located within the Headquarters 1 Division camp at Khaw. Although officers were still sent to England for staff training, it was hoped gradually to build up a pool of Jordanian-trained staff officers, who would be able to fill some at least of the staff appointments at the various headquarters from brigades upwards.

Glubb had always been determined, however quickly the army had to grow to meet its operational tasks, that he would not accept the second-rate; the care and thought given to training at all levels in the Arab Legion went a long way to meet this ideal.

APPENDIX
Equivalent Arab Legion/British Army Ranks

Arab Legion	British Army	Courtesy Title
Al Fariq	Lieutenant-General	Pasha
Amir al Liwa	Major-General	
Zaim	Brigadier	
Qaimakam	Colonel	
Qaid	Lieutenant-Colonel	Bey
Wakil Qaid	Major	
Rais	Captain	
Mulazim Awal	Lieutenant	
Mulazim Thani	Second Lieutenant	
Morasha	Cadet	Effendi
Waqil	Warrant Officer	
Naqib	Staff Sergeant	
Naib	Sergeant	
Areef	Corporal	
Jundi Awal	Lance-Corporal	
Jundi Thani	Private	

The Plates

A Desert Patrol

This is a bedouin soldier, perhaps of the Howeitat tribe from South Jordan which gave so much support to T. E. Lawrence during the 1914–18 war, when their chief was the famous warrior Auda Abu Tay. Shown here in full dress, a uniform of khaki drill is worn. It was cut in the same manner as ordinary bedouin dress, with long robes reaching almost to the ground. A red sash is worn, together with a red revolver lanyard on the right shoulder, a belt and bandolier full of ammunition and a silver dagger in the front of the belt. Normally when on patrol in the desert the soldier would not wear the long white 'cuffs' falling from his sleeves. He holds a long bamboo cane in his right hand, which helps him to steer his somewhat unpredictable mount. The scarlet saddle cloth is in fact a cloak or mantle of fine cloth, lined with sheepskin, and it is this which serves as protection against the cold desert nights. The saddlery is decorated in bedouin style, with a fantasia of coloured woollen ornamentation. Equipment includes a Mark IV Lee-Enfield rifle and a ·38 pistol, the latter is suspended from the right arm and therefore cannot be seen.

B1 Colonel (Qaimakam), 1955

In full winter dress, this officer is a *Qaimakam* (or colonel) of bedouin origin. His neck decoration is the Order of El Nahda (Third Class), and he also holds the Order of El Istiqlal (Fourth Class). These two decorations are divided into five classes, the fifth being reserved for other ranks, fourth for junior officers and so on.

From a portrait taken by the author at the Opening of Parliament in Amman, 1 November 1955.

B2 Commander, Mounted Bodyguard, 1955

This officer is a *Rais* (or captain) and wears the full dress of the Royal Bodyguard. The tunic is red with dark blue facings, and the breeches are also dark blue.

From a colour slide taken at the Arab Legion Mounted Sports near Zerka late in 1955.

B3 Major-General (Qaid el Firqa), 1955

This officer wears his winter service dress, with black leather Sam Browne belt and shoes. His decorations include the Order of El Istiqlal of Jordan (Star and Sash) and the C.B. (neck decoration).

From a portrait of Major-General S. A. Cooke, C.B., O.B.E., taken by the author at the Opening of Parliament in Amman, 1 November 1955.

C1 Lieutenant-Colonel (Qaid), 9th Infantry Regiment, 1955

The uniform is the khaki drill service dress as worn during the summer months. The red and green lanyard and badges on the epaulette straps are regimental, the latter being surmounted by the normal *Jeish-el-Arabi* badge of white metal. The Sam Browne belt and shoes are of black leather, not brown as in the British service at the time. The pistol, a luger, carried as shown is not regulation. The head-dress is the dark blue *sedara* (or forage cap), with a red crown and piping and ornamented with the Arab Legion cap badge. This officer is one of those seconded from the British Army. At the time, four of the ten regular battalions of the Arab Legion were commanded by British officers.

From a colour slide of *Qaid* P. Young, D.S.O., M.C., taken at Zerka in the summer of 1955.

C2 Standard-Bearer, 7th Infantry Regiment, 1953

A junior officer in full dress, bearing the Regiment's Colour (*el alam*), old pattern, at the Arab Legion Day Parade. Only ranks of Warrant Officer and above wore ties.

C3 Colour-Sergeant (Naguib), 9th Infantry Regiment, 1955

Wearing the full-dress summer uniform of khaki drill, this senior N.C.O is a bedouin, and one of the Guard of Honour for the President of Lebanon as indicated by the wearing of white gloves. All non-commissioned officers wear stripes of the British style, but the metal stars and crowns of senior N.C.O.s and officers are of Arabic design. He is armed with a Mark III Lee-Enfield rifle, and carries his bayonet on the left hip – this being concealed by the knot of his crimson sash.

From a colour slide taken by the author at Amman airport in 1955.

D Trooper, Mounted Police (Fursan), 1955
This trooper wears his summer uniform of khaki drill service dress. He has black leather equipment, belt and bandolier, and is armed with the British Mark III Lee-Enfield. Note that the police, like the National Guard, wear a *shemagh* distinctive from the rest of the Arab Legion. The silver cap badge of the Arab Legion is the same for soldiers and police, while a different badge of yellow metal is worn by the National Guard. The horse appears to be a tough country-bred arab of about fourteen hands, perhaps rather small by British standards for the load he has to carry, but nevertheless well up to his work.

From a colour slide taken by the author near Amman on 18 July 1955.

E1 Drummer, Arab Legion Band, c. 1953
The winter battle-dress is of the standard British pattern of the day, adorned with blue epaulettes and aiguillette. Belt and gaiters are also of the British pattern but blancoed. The *shemagh* and *agal* are the normal Arab Legion issue, the former being tucked into the back of the belt to keep it in place. The badge on the *agal* is that worn by all the regular personnel of the Arab Legion. The drum was one of a set bought from Messrs. Potter & Co. of Aldershot in the 1950s, and is metal with the badge and title emblazoned on it. This soldier appears to be a non-bedouin Jordanian Arab.

From a coloured photograph by Major R. Young and reproduced in The Arab Legion Calendar.

E2 Cadet, Cadet Training School, Amman, 1955
This cadet wears British battle-dress with white gorget patches while at Cadet School, but when he leaves he will wear silver bars on his shoulder. He differs little from his British counterpart of the

period, except for the *sedara* (forage cap) and the Arab Legion badge on his epaulette strap. A cadet has to serve in a regiment for three years before being promoted second-lieutenant – always supposing he passes his promotion exam.

E3 Drum-Major, Arab Legion Band, c. 1955
The drum-major, probably selected for his height (!), is only a *Jundi Awal* (lance-corporal). He wears his winter uniform, which is British battle-dress, buttoned to the neck, with the usual Arab Legion badges, and ornamented with blue epaulettes and lanyard. The colour of these latter indicates that this drum-major is a member of the blue band, there being three bands in the Arab Legion – the red, the blue and the green.

F1 Corporal (Areef), Circassian Bodyguard, 1955
This bodyguard was raised by King Abdallah, but by 1955 it was small in numbers and its personnel, despite their soldierly, not to say ferocious, appearance were becoming rather elderly. Their handsome uniform, with *yataghan* (dagger) and cartridge-cases, seems to have been inspired by the cossacks of the old Imperial Russian Army.

From a colour slide taken by the author at the Opening of Parliament in Amman, 1 November 1955.

F2 Trooper, Jundi Than's 2nd Armoured Car Regiment, 1955
This soldier is dressed in British battle-dress, which is his winter uniform. He wears the *shemagh* and *agal* and the badge on his right arm is regimental. It is his duty to care for the regimental mascot, a hawk, which was introduced when *Qaid* (Lieut.-Colonel), now Major-General, J. D. Lunt was commanding the unit. The Despatch Rider's gauntlets are worn, of course, as a protection against the bird's talons.

F3 Trooper, Camel Corps, 1955
The uniform is that worn by the Desert Police (*Badieh*) during the winter; summer uniform as worn in full dress is of khaki drill. The equipment is of dark red leather. The soldier wears his pistol bullets (·38) over his left shoulder, and his rifle bullets (·303) in the bandolier around his waist.

The white metal badge on the right of his chest bears his army number.

From a colour slide taken by the author in Amman in November 1955.

G *Trooper, Household Cavalry Squadron, 1955*
This trooper was photographed by the author at the Opening of Parliament in Amman on 1 November 1955. He wears the full-dress red coat and navy blue breeches of the Household Cavalry, which was not a bedouin unit, but recruited from among the *fellahin* or *haderi* inhabitants of Jordan. All the horses were greys, not unlike large New Forest ponies, and the men were armed with lances made of aluminium.

H1 *Corporal (Areef), Arab Legion Engineers, c. 1954*
The uniform is the standard battle-dress with belt and gaiters, all of British pattern. The N.C.O.'s chevrons have been whitened with blanco. The white metal badge on the epaulette straps was worn throughout the Arab Legion, and bore the words '*Jeish-el-Arabi*' (Arab Army) in Arabic characters. The blue and red badge above the chevrons is that of the Arab Legion Engineers. From his appearance and style of wearing his *shemagh* this corporal could be a bedouin, but as there were few, if any, in the Engineers, he is probably a *haderi*.

From a coloured photograph taken by Major R. Young and reproduced in The Arab Legion Calendar.

H2 *Constable, Police, 1955*
The blue serge service dress is as worn on traffic duty in winter, while in summer the uniform would be khaki drill battle-dress. He appears to be armed with a Colt or Browning automatic. Note the distinctive spiked head-dress of the Arab Legion Police. The web equipment has been adapted from that acquired from Great Britain. The collar-badge gives the policeman's army number.

From a slide taken by the author in Amman in 1955.

H3 *Private, National Guard (Haris el Watani), 1954*
This soldier was photographed by the author in an Observation Post on the frontier between Jordan and Israel. He belonged to a battalion that had been mobilized, as opposed to the National Guard raised solely for the protection of frontier villages. He was of typical Palestinian *haderi* stock, not of bedouin extraction. His khaki drill battle-dress is of British style. About his waist is a bandolier of ·303 cartridges, and his khaki *shemagh* and yellow metal badge are peculiar to the National Guard.